The Political Economy and Ethics of Debt Financing

This book takes a fresh look at an age-old controversy in ethics and political economy that stretches right back to Aristotle: the morality and the economics of debt financing, or the charging of interest on loans. It endeavours to show the immense relevance of those ancient debates in the contemporary economy.

Outside of countries which practise Islam and Islamic finance, the charging of interest is taken completely for granted today and little or no thought is devoted to its morality or economic and social impacts. This book argues that in fact the question of the morality of charging interest is still debatable and deserves to be considered anew in the 21st century for the light it can shine on certain salient contemporary sources of economic malaise. This book will first of all review the ancient debates on these questions stretching back to Aristotle seeking to restate the concerns in terms of contemporary economic theories and realities. It will also then delve into the current practices in respect of lending of all kinds that can be found in those Islamic countries and financial institutions which endeavour to follow the prohibition of *riba* (charging of any kind of interest). This will be contrasted with the impact of interest and debt financing in the contemporary non-Islamic economies arguing that debt financing of businesses promotes greater rates of bankruptcy over the business cycle and that the charging of interest on loans for current consumption purposes will over time increase inequality and inequitable concentration of wealth in societies where it is practised. It will also be shown how in a system without predetermined interest charges problems of exponentially exploding government debt could largely and neatly be avoided by linking bondholder rewards to levels of fiscal proceeds of states.

This book will be of significant interest to readers in ethics, moral philosophy and political economy as well as to policymakers and thinkers grappling with issues around debt burdens (public and private), inequality and fairness.

Patrick O'Sullivan is Adjunct Professor at the University of Warsaw; Visiting Professor at Università di Parma; and Visiting Research Faculty at Thammasat University Business School, Bangkok. He contributes an elective course on Geopolitics and Business annually on the Judge Business School University of Cambridge MBA and has in addition taught on university courses in France, UK, Poland, Estonia, Georgia and Thailand. He has acted as editor for two collected volumes on the ethics of business and of finance and has written numerous articles on business ethics and critical political economy.

Paolo Ricci is Full Professor of Business Administration and Public Accountability in the Department of Political Science, University of Naples Federico II, Italy. He has taught at several universities, including Roma LUMSA, Roma Tre and Sannio University. He coordinated international research projects, and he is a member of numerous editorial committees. He is the author of over 200 scientific publications mainly on issues concerning public sector governance and accountability, responsibility and social reporting.

Routledge Frontiers of Political Economy

Government and Economic Growth in the 21st Century
A Classical Liberal Response
Edited by Juan E. Castañeda

Political Economy in Middle East and North-Africa
Why Institutions, Rents and Power Matter in Economic Reforms
Rachid Mira

How Economists Think
A Kantian Interpretation of Mainstream Economics
Steven Buccola

Economic Populism and Institutional Reform
Emre Ünal

Capital, Entrepreneurship and Management
A New Austrian Theory of Organizations
Thierry Aimar

Capitalism as Megamachine
A New Historical, Legal and Political Approach
Jacques Richard

A Financial Theory of the Business Cycle
Net Present Value and Fractional Reserve Banking
Fuller and Young

International Taxation and Capitalism
A Heterodox Economics Perspective
Andres Blanco

For more information about this series, please visit: www.routledge.com/Routledge-Frontiers-of-Political-Economy/book-series/SE0345

The Political Economy and Ethics of Debt Financing

The Brutality of the Charging of Interest on Loans

Patrick O'Sullivan and Paolo Ricci

Routledge
Taylor & Francis Group
LONDON AND NEW YORK

First published 2025
by Routledge
4 Park Square, Milton Park, Abingdon, Oxon OX14 4RN

and by Routledge
605 Third Avenue, New York, NY 10158

Routledge is an imprint of the Taylor & Francis Group, an informa business

British Library Cataloguing-in-Publication Data
A catalogue record for this book is available from the British Library

ISBN: 9781032900674 (hbk)
ISBN: 9781032900704 (pbk)
ISBN: 9781003546030 (ebk)

DOI: 10.4324/9781003546030

Typeset in Times New Roman
by codeMantra

Contents

1 The growing contemporary challenge of indebtedness

That the world today has been facing a range of major debt crises over at least the past 15 years will hardly be disputed. In addition to the high-profile case of Greek sovereign debt which almost led to the breakup of the European single currency, there are currently in Europe public sector gross debt to GDP ratios such as those of Belgium (106%), France (112%), Greece (159%), Italy (139%), Spain (106%) and Portugal (95%) which are arguably unsustainable in the long run (at least as long as the payment of interest on the debt is demanded – of this much more will be said later in the volume); and outside of the Euro zone there are the cases of Japan (255%), USA (123%) and Laos (116%) just to take some examples (all figures are for 2024 from the IMF).[1] But the debt crises are not just confined to the public sector: there is a less well-publicised and less-researched crisis of private sector consumer indebtedness (with aggregate household debt to GDP ratios well in excess of 60% and even over 100% in certain cases)[2] which while not posing quite the same threat of unsustainability as public sector debt is nonetheless acting as a macroeconomic brake on consumer demand in many advanced countries. It is also as we shall see in this book rendering the distribution of wealth increasingly unequal and arguably more inequitable in those countries where it looms large. The details of these diverse debt burdens and their nefarious politico-economic impacts will be presented in the coming chapters.

The purpose of this book is to invite a radical reflection on the role which is played in the unfolding of these crises by the practice of charging interest on loans and to suggest that serious consideration should be given to the complete abolition of all interest payments on loans. This apparently radical suggestion will of course be met with a strong resistance precisely because of the fairly brutal upheaval of contemporary economic practices which it would entail, but it should be borne in mind that the current set-up of debt financing with interest payments is generating its own brutality in the form of intolerable unforgiving debt burdens as will be explained later in this book.

There are those who at this point will already be inclined to set this book aside saying that this is "pure socialism" (as Milton Friedman once described the imperative of company social responsibility)[3] or that it is just hopelessly

DOI: 10.4324/9781003546030-1

unrealistic. However, before being tempted to such a peremptory dismissal of the idea let it be recalled that Islamic finance works (or at least is supposed to work) on this as a central principle; and that no less an ancient authority whose moral thinking has had a huge influence on Western ethical thinking, namely Aristotle, roundly and unambiguously condemned all charging of interest on loans as immoral extortion and as incompatible with natural law. Hence a financial system without interest is not only conceivable, it can work in practice (Islamic finance) and at least for those who would follow Aristotelian ethics, it is morally preferable.

The purpose is not to suggest that the elimination of interest on loans is some kind of panacea that will somehow cure all of the ills of the financial sector and eliminate the persistently recurring financial crises which are often so profoundly damaging to the real economy ushering in periods of deep depression such as those which followed the 1929 or 2008 financial crashes to cite the most glaring examples. There will still be a need for much more imaginative regulation, for the reining in untrammelled personal greed and for more socially responsible behaviour by all actors in the financial sector. These themes are well rehearsed in the volume on the *Philosophy Politics and Economics of Finance in the 21st Century* (2015).[4] There is also the on-going heated debate among economists and politicians regarding the full range of effects and the relative merits of austerity policies which is an integral part of the debate on the appropriate future of finance. Aware of these discussions and of their importance we are in no way trying to suggest in this book a single miracle solution which will cure all financial ills. But what we are saying is that one key element among an array of policies to address the dysfunctions of contemporary finance could be the elimination of the charging of interest on loans; the elimination of debt financing in effect.

This book thus invites a radical reflection on a sector which is not accustomed to see itself called into question and which as we shall see is littered with all manner of questionable dogmas in respect of interest payment and risk. Central to our whole discussion is a moral presumption which we freely acknowledge and will defend in detail in later chapters: that finance as every other sector of the economy should first and foremost serve the common good, it should contribute to the well-being of all in a society. Of course financiers, well versed in certain aspects of Adam Smith's work, will claim that in pursuing their own narrow self-interests they are thereby promoting the well-being of all; but that, let us be blunt, is nothing but a fairy tale especially in the financial sector. For the Smithian magic of the Invisible Hand to work there has to be perfect competition in all markets and access for all actors to perfect (or at least near perfect *and* symmetric) information regarding the future. These assumptions are not even remotely approximated over most of the world of finance. Not only are there huge concentrations of power in a small number of big global banks, it is now well known that these and other actors in the financial sector have been systematically seeking to rig various interest rates and exchange rates.[5] Moreover the by now well-established (even if not mainstream) field of behavioural finance[6] has drawn attention to the irreducible subjectivity and non-rationality of expectations of the future and hence of all saving and investment decisions which after all cannot avoid taking a view about what the uncertain future will hold. In short the central theories of contemporary finance such as the Capital Asset Pricing Model and the Efficient Markets Hypothesis with their assumptions of well-informed agents forming strictly rational expectations[7] are what in the terms of critical social theory we would call pure ideology. That is to say that they represent a fictional narrative with little or no basis in reality but which serves the interests of some particular social group propounding it. And yet the whole edifice of the theory and practice of the contemporary financial system depends critically and must assume the validity of this fictional narrative.

It is interesting to remark in this context that at the height of the discussions in 2015 between the Greek government and its various creditors led by the *Troika*,[8] the Greek Prime Minister Alexis Tsipras spoke of the deep ideological differences between his government and that of Angela Merkel's CDU-CSU coalition in Germany. Rarely made explicit but almost certainly having a key influence on that German-Greek stand-off was the implicit German tendency to identify all debt as bad: in the German language the words for debt and for (moral) guilt are the same (*Schuld*). But when Tsipras spoke of the ideological differences no doubt what he had in mind was the classic left-right divide between socialists on the left and conservatives and/or free market fundamentalists on the right, or in more classical sociological terms, between labour and capital. We will argue in this book that was not the most pertinent ideological divide in the early 21st century, and in many European states at least that old dividing line has been surpassed as left of centre social democratic and right of centre liberal or conservative parties become almost indistinguishable in terms of their economic policies. Rather the relevant divide today (and one which has brutally been in evidence in the Greek sovereign debt crisis) is that between *creditors* and *debtors*. We will examine the power dynamics of this divide and our thesis is that the elimination of interest on loans would offer a much-needed rebalancing of the power relations inherent in this relationship and could help to ensure that finance instead of being utterly and narrowly self-serving as at present serves *both* itself *and* the society at large. We do not underestimate the challenges of such a rebalancing firstly not only because of the entrenched and largely covert lobbying power of the financial sector but also because of the widespread cultural perception of those who go bankrupt (whether at individual or corporate level) as untrustworthy failures or "losers" even if in many cases the bankruptcy occurs for reasons largely or entirely outside of their control (natural disasters or macroeconomic slumps). By contrast creditors bask in virtuous self-righteous esteem and even label themselves occasionally as "*business angels*". Resetting the power balance between creditors and debtors will have to contend with such implicit stereotypes which will not fade away rapidly or easily.

This book will be organised as follows. Chapters 2–4 will examine in depth the moral questions surrounding the charging of interest on loans setting this within the economic understanding of the phenomenon and in doing so will examine critically some of the (usually circular) arguments offered by economists to explain the phenomenon of interest. Ideas of service to society and social contract, now fairly familiar in business ethics will be applied to the financial sector in particular to structure the critical ethical discussion of the charging of interest; does this practice really provide a service to society or is it simply the first cousin of back street lenders' extortive practices?

After the theoretical ethical discussion which will suggest the moral imperative of abolishing all interest on loans Chapters 5–7 will give an outline of how a financial system without interest could work in practice drawing in part on the procedures of contemporary Islamic finance. For business lending a system of risk sharing whereby the lender participates in the eventual profits *or* losses of the business borrower is proposed and it is argued that over the period of a typical business cycle such a system would produce a much superior macroeconomic impact in terms of employment and bankruptcies than an interest-based system of debt financing for business. In Chapters 6 and 7 the question of zero interest financing of lending to private consumers (as opposed to businesses) and to governments is examined, and in practice this is a lot more challenging than the case of business lending. Whereas a bank or other financial actor lending to a business can replace interest with a share in profits/losses as a reward for lending, in the case of lending to consumers the only cases where any income stream is generated are mortgage lending which generates a rental (or implicit rental foregone) income to the real estate owner and student loans which (usually) lead to higher incomes. Also in the case of the government borrowing no such flow of profits is generated except in the case of certain major infrastructure projects of the government (which by generating economic growth can boost tax revenues); or perhaps in cases where government deficits are run with a view to stimulating an economy in the depths of severe recession and where the resulting multiplier and accelerator effects on aggregate demand produce a strong recovery of real output and with that a significant increase in tax revenues. We will draw some radical conclusions: for private consumers all lending should be entirely banned apart from mortgage lending and student loans. As regards lending to governments except for the case of big infrastructure projects which will boost overall productivity or for countercyclical recovery in the face of deep recession such borrowing should be entirely banned and even in the case of infrastructure projects, the financing should be on the basis of profit and loss sharing and not on the basis of interest.

Returns on lending to governments for countercyclical purposes could be linked to the evolution of gross tax revenues rather than being based on fixed bond coupons. As with the proposals for business financing the macroeconomic impact of these measures will be thought through and critically assessed and it will be argued that they are surprisingly positive in their long-term socio-economic impact.

Chapter 8 will present a detailed discussion of the effects of an interest-based system of finance on the distribution of income and wealth both within economies and at global level. It will be argued that when stripped down to its bare essentials no system more designed to render the distribution of wealth ever more unequal could be imagined. In essence in an interest-based system "*to the one who has, more will be given, and he will have an abundance, but from the one who has not, even what he has will be taken away*".[9] This is quite patently what happens in the case of any lending which does not generate a new income flow; hence all private consumer borrowing other than mortgages and much government borrowing.

In Chapter 9, this book will conclude with a call to action in which we will argue that it is time to leave behind some of the stale old ideological debates of the 20th century to recognise that the real challenge today is to ensure that the financial system duly revamped on a zero interest basis properly serves society rather than serving itself. We will look at some of the specific contemporary challenges of finance and explain how the zero interest system proposed can help to address those dysfunctions. It will be suggested that there is no hope whatever of avoiding sooner or later a default on the sovereign debt of Greece, Belgium, Spain, Portugal, Italy and probably also France and Ireland unless all interest payments in the outstanding (and any new) debts are entirely eliminated (and that in nominal and not just real terms). Moreover it will be argued that any new borrowing by government (or by public-private partnerships) should observe the unfairly maligned Golden Rule of Public Finance which stipulates that governments should only borrow to finance growth-inducing infrastructural investments; and the returns to financiers should be related to attained growth in tax revenues which in turn will typically reflect economic growth in the borrowing country (unless major changes of tax rates and coverage have occurred). As for the complete elimination of borrowing by private consumers other than mortgage lending, it will be argued that while this would no doubt generate a short-term collapse in aggregate consumer spending as consumers adjust to a new reality whereby they save first and thereafter consume within their means, in the longer term the effects will, we believe, be highly beneficial to society at large in a whole range of ways; less inequality, less personal stress … and more loanable funds available for productive business or government infrastructural investments.

We are under no illusions as to the huge inertia of vested interests such proposals will encounter (for there is no sector as inherently conservative, politically well-connected and self-serving as finance); but we believe that the effort must be made. The signs of a deep economic and political malaise are there for all to see throughout the world; participation in democratic elections is almost everywhere on the decline while politicians are increasingly seen as untrustworthy and irretrievably corrupt.[10]

Whether this is a social media-induced exaggeration or not is beside the point as it is the perception that gives rise to the distrust; and while the resulting political malaise is not exclusively due to the world financial system as currently constituted, there can be no doubt that a system that generates so automatically increasing inequality of wealth, that leads to the imposition of swingeing austerity by creditors on debtors and that flies directly in the face of a central moral principle of Aristotelian and Islamic ethics is one of the contributing causes to that deep malaise.[11] We believe therefore that this decline of trust in democracies is not just a matter of political and moral decadence, there is also a significant component that arises from disillusionment with the power imbalances that have emerged in the contemporary economic system dominated as it is by a market fundamentalism which exalts antagonism and greed in the name of economic freedom to accumulate and (a caricature of) competition and which has lost sight of the role and importance of cooperation among human beings in achieving certain social goals and in facing certain common shared problems (such as climate change most obviously).[12] In a system in which people are in constant acquisitive competition against each other and where economic inequalities are everywhere rising[13] can it be surprising that this eventually spills over into outright warfare?

Notes

1 For a comprehensive picture on gross public sector debt levels in 2023, see International Monetary Fund (IMF) data mapper website at https://www.imf.org/external/datamapper/GGXWDG_NGDP@WEO/OEMDC/ADVEC/WEOWORLD accessed 9 July 2024.

2 For private sector debt levels, see IMF Fiscal Affairs Department (2023) *Global Debt Monitor*, IMF, Washington DC; and also the IMF data maps available at https://www.imf.org/external/datamapper/HH_LS@GDD/SWE/AUS/CAN/DEU/USA/GBR accessed 9 July 2024.

3 Friedman, M. (1970). The social responsibility of business is to increase profits. *New York Times Magazine*, 13 September 1970.

4 O'Sullivan, P., Allington, N., & Esposito, M. (2015). *The Philosophy Politics and Economics of Finance in the 21st Century: From Hubris to Disgrace*. London: Routledge.

5 We are referring to the scandal of the rigging of the London Interbank lending rate (LIBOR). For a good summary, see Vaughn, L., & Finch, G. (2017). The bankers who fixed the world's most important number. *The Guardian*. London, 18 January 2017.

6 This is now a significant field built around ideas first propounded by John Maynard Keynes and developed in more recent times for example in the works of Daniel Kahnemann, Robert Schiller and Hyman Minski.

7 For readers trained in economics or philosophy we cannot pass without noting the vicious circularity inherent in the definition often given of rational expectations as "expectations formed objectively in the light of … economic theory"!

8 Troika (the Gang of Three) refers here to the IMF, European Central Bank and European Commission.

9 The quotation is from the Gospel of St Matthew (English standard version) 25:29.

10 See various reports produced in recent years on the gradual but unmistakable fall of trust in politicians who are increasingly seen as furthering their own personal interests rather than any kind of common good. For example Institute of Public Policy Research UK (2021). *Trust in Politicians at Lowest Level on Record*, available at https://www.ippr.org/news-and-media/press-releases/revealed-trust-in-politicians-at-lowest-level-on-record/ accessed 11 July 2024. At a more international level, see: OECD (2022). *Building Trust to reinforce Democracy*. Paris: OECD. On declining voter participation in democratic elections, see International Institute for Democracy and Electoral assistance IDEA (2016) Voter Turnout Trends around the World, Strömsborg Sweden. What is striking in this report is that the phenomenon of declining participation is across all continents.

11 Lest we forget the Second World War grew ultimately from the ravages and inequities that followed from the financial mania of the 1920s and the subsequent Great Crash of 1929. That was not of course the only factor but the dysfunctions of the world financial system of the 1920s and 1930s made their contribution to that disastrous conflagration. In our own day the malaise generated by inequity has turned up on Europe's doorstep in an intriguing way: migrant flows towards the rich advanced economies of Western Europe where there are job opportunities.

12 Similar arguments can be found in: Wolf, M. (2023). *The Crisis of Democratic Capitalism*. London: Allen Lane Penguin Press. Wolf also argues that the crises of contemporary democratic regimes in the face of populisms of various stripes have clearly identifiable economic as well as political roots. See also Monbiot, G., & Hutchison, P. (2024). *The Invisible Doctrine: The Secret History of Neo-liberalism*. London: Allen Lane Penguin Press; passim but especially chapters 7 and 8.

13 See: Piketty, T. (2014). *Capitalism in the 21st Century*. Boston: Harvard University Press: *passim*. See also the detailed database of the World Inequality Lab in: Chancel, L., Piketty, T., Saez, E., & Zucman, G. (2023). *World Inequality Report*, available at https://wir2022.wid.world/www-site/uploads/2021/12/WorldInequalityReport2022_Full_Report.pdf accessed 11 July 2024.

Bibliography

Chancel, L., Piketty, T., Saez, E., & Zucman, G. (2023). *World Inequality Report*, available at https://wir2022.wid.world/www-site/uploads/2021/12/WorldInequality-Report2022_Full_Report.pdf accessed 11 July 2024.

Friedman, M. (1970). The social responsibility of business is to increase profits. *New York Times Magazine*, 13 September 1970.

IMF (2024). Data mapper website at https://www.imf.org/external/datamapper/GGX-WDG_NGDP@WEO/OEMDC/ADVEC/WEOWORLD accessed 9 July 2024.

IMF Fiscal Affairs Department (2023). *Global Debt Monitor*, IMF, Washington DC; and also the IMF data maps, available at https://www.imf.org/external/datamapper/HH_LS@GDD/SWE/AUS/CAN/DEU/USA/GBR accessed 9 July 2024.

Institute of Public Policy Research UK (2021). *Trust in Politicians at Lowest Level on Record*, available at https://www.ippr.org/news-and-media/press-releases/revealed-trust-in-politicians-at-lowest-level-on-record/ accessed 11 July 2024.

Monbiot, G., & Hutchison, P. (2024). *The Invisible Doctrine: The Secret History of Neo-liberalism*. London: Allen Lane Penguin Press.

OECD (2022). *Building Trust to Reinforce Democracy*. Paris: OECD.

O'Sullivan, P., Allington, N., & Esposito, M. (2015). *The Philosophy Politics and Economics of Finance in the 21st Century: From Hubris to Disgrace*. London: Routledge.

Piketty, T. (2014). *Capitalism in the 21st Century*. Boston: Harvard University Press.

Vaughn, L., & Finch, G. (2017). The bankers who fixed the world's most important number. *The Guardian*, 18 January 2017. Available at https://www.theguardian.com/business/2017/jan/18/libor-scandal-the-bankers-who-fixed-the-worlds-most-important-number accessed 28 October 2024.

Wolf, M. (2023). *The Crisis of Democratic Capitalism*. London: Allen Lane Penguin Press.

2 The morality of the charging of interest on loans

The ancient and mediaeval moral philosophical debate

It may seem arcane to many readers to seek to launch once again the ancient debate about the morality of interest and usury, of the charging of interest on loans. Is not the charging of interest pervasive and inevitable, have not economists closed that debate with their demonstration of the key allocative role of interest in the macroeconomy and is not the manipulation of interest rates the central policy lever of central banks the world over? Well, er, yes indeed to each of the points in the last sentence. But then the existence of slavery was also regarded for centuries as economically inevitable if not a pillar of the economic system. Our point is not that the charging of interest is a form of slavery although when loan repayment takes the form of debt bondage it becomes very close to slavery. More figuratively but equally telling we may recall the insightful words of the then president of Uruguay, José Mujica when addressing a meeting of the G20 in Rio de Janeiro in 2012:

> Today, man does not govern the forces he has unleashed, but rather, it is these forces that govern man; and life … My fellow workers, fought hard for the 8 hour workday. And now they are making that 6 hours. But the person who works 6 hours, gets two jobs, therefore, he works longer than before. But why? Because he needs to make monthly payments for: the motorcycle, the car, more and more payments, and when he's done with that, he realizes he is a rheumatic old man, like me, and his life is already over. And one asks this question: is this the fate of human life?[1]

Our aim is not however to argue that all debt involves slavery but rather the much more general reflection that practices which are pervasive and seemingly economically inevitable may nonetheless be subjected to serious moral criticism; and it found to be morally wanting there may be a strong argument to end those practices with a view to making a better world. So just because the charging of interest on loans is widely accepted and a central lever of contemporary monetary policy, this does not put the practice beyond the pale of criticism or does it render the possibility of an alternative necessarily utopian as we shall see in later chapters of this book which discuss how an economic

DOI: 10.4324/9781003546030-2

system without interest could work. Equally even if in the emergent field of "ethical finance" which urges creditors and investors to place their loanable funds in projects which are environmentally and socially sustainable one does not find any significant discussion of the morality of charging of interest on such "ethical" loans, this does not mean that the question of the morality of charging on interest on such "ethical" loans or on any loans cannot be raised. We will argue that there is more to "ethical finance" than simply selecting laudable sustainable investment projects: there are also more fundamental issues regarding the distribution of power between creditors and debtors implicit in contemporary interest-based debt finance.

In any case the practices of charging interest are not all wholeheartedly and unreservedly approved by all today. There are certain practices which remain to this very day a matter of lively moral debate even in the most market fundamentalist of countries: practices such as back street loan sharking with exorbitant interest rates which to many seem to be pure extortion of the vulnerable; or debt bondage where a person's labour time is unpaid being taken instead in repayment of a loan (again at exorbitant interest rates). And lest anyone be under any illusion about the extortionate nature of these loans the annualised percentage interest rate (APR) on such lending is typically between 100% and 1,500%.[2] There is also of course the longstanding prohibition of the charging of interest in Islam and so in Islamic finance.

So without any apology for being anachronistic or antediluvian we will now review the ancient and modern debates on the topic of the morality of the charging of interest on loans.

Aristotle and other European ancients

As with so many of the great moral and political debates that have engaged the minds of man the first philosophical argumentation in Europe on the topic of the morality of interest can be traced back to ancient Greece and to the work of Aristotle in particular.[3] In his *Nicomachean Ethics* Aristotle developed what was the first systematic treatise on moral questions in Western thought; and in his *Politics* moral themes are interwoven with considerations of economics and politics to yield in effect a work of critical political economy.[4] This work is imbued with the philosophy of Natural Law, the view whereby there is an inherent natural order or natural harmony in the universe and that harmony is in itself good. Indeed in ancient Greek the word for harmony and for the universe is the same, *kosmos*; and the *kosmos* is thought of as inherently one, true, *good* and beautiful.[5] Hence for Aristotle the good life or a truly fulfilled human existence will be a life lived in harmony with the greater natural order of the universe, in accordance with natural laws; so what is natural is good. Now of course there can be a great deal of debate about what exactly is natural for human beings or what is human nature, and the great existentialist thinker

Jean-Paul Sartre actually argued that freely choosing human beings define their own nature through their life choices.[6] But our purpose here is not to enter into debates about natural law as such but rather to illustrate what Aristotle had to say about charging interest on loans; and in that Aristotle was unequivocal: the practice is unnatural and therefore *ipso facto* morally bad. Aristotle thought of any form of profit-making through trade and commerce as a dubious gaining from other people (*chrematistic* exchange) no doubt because he thought of trade and commerce as a zero sum game where one person's gain must mean another's loss. Following from that (clearly mistaken) presumption Aristotle went on to make the famous assertion in his *Politics* that

> The most hated sort [of chrematistic moneymaking], and with the greatest reason, is usury, which makes a gain out of money itself, and not from the natural use of it. For money was intended to be used in exchange, but not to increase at interest. And this term Usury which means the birth of money from money, is applied to the breeding of money, because the offspring resembles the parent. Wherefore of all modes of making money this is the most unnatural.[7]

This is what Walsh and Lynch have dubbed the objection from barrenness.[8] Money is essentially barren in itself, incapable of yielding 'offspring'. Now although Aristotle was surely wrong to presume that in trade and commerce there must always be losers as well as gainers (i.e. that trade and exchange are always zero sum games) this argument about the barrenness specifically of money may well have a point. For it is strictly true that money cannot entirely by itself produce more money unless we assume a system which already involves interest; and since what we are debating is the moral acceptability of such a system, to assume that interest already exists involves a vicious circularity. Outside of a system with interest money is indeed strictly barren; it is only when money is invested in a form of physical or human capital that it can provide a return. Money per se is **not** capital; it is merely an instrument of exchange which *can* be transformed into a form of real capital if the holder of the money so wishes *but* it could equally well be spent on an immediate consumption binge, in which case there is no return, no net creation of new value. This is the core of truth in the Aristotelian assertion *that* money is essentially barren in itself. Any possible ethical basis for payment of interest on money lent can only emerge when the money has been transformed (used to buy) real capital of various kinds. Money cannot therefore, strictly speaking, be considered to be a factor of production and can only become such as and when it is transformed into one of the real factors of production (labour, land, equipment or research-based know-how).

The Aristotelian view permeated also the prevalent view of the taking of interest in ancient Rome and it is from this time that the word "usury" (Latin *usuria*) dates. At this point it is perhaps useful to define precisely the etymological difference between usury and interest, a distinction which is not always well appreciated in contemporary discussions. Usury means the charging of an excess unearned payment when a loan is repaid; taking back *more* than what was given. Essentially this can be seen as pure extortion (and that is certainly how Aristotle saw it because of the barrenness argument). By contrast the term "interest" derives from the Latin verb *intereo* which means (among other things) to enter into losses or a state of ruin. Hence the payment of *interest* on a loan means recompensing the lender for losses incurred through the lending; it means giving back exactly what one was lent whole and intact but not a jot more. The Romans who of course had a flourishing commercial empire actually made a rather interesting distinction in Roman Law between two different types of loan: the *commodatum* and the *mutuum.*[9] In the *commodatum* what is lent is an object (in effect a piece of capital equipment) which will not be destroyed or entirely used up when being used by the borrower: in the terminology of economic theory the *commodatum* involves the loan of real capital strictly so-called. Here the capital lent must be restored whole and entire to the lender at the end of the agreed loan period; any damages beyond normal wear and tear must be made good to the lender and this is precisely what *interest* strictly means: the making good of damages. There could be no question of the lender requiring anything more than the restoration of damage to the real capital lent; to do so would be usurious, asking back more than what was lent and was regarded as illegal extortion in Roman Law. In the case of a *mutuum* what is lent is consumable and so there can be no way for the borrower to give back exactly what was lent precisely because the object lent will be consumed. So the borrower is required in Roman Law to restore to the lender at the end of the agreed loan period goods of equivalent value but *not* any more than that. In the *mutuum* therefore there can be no question of interest strictly speaking while any usury is regarded as unlawful and indeed as immoral. For the Romans there was no doubt that lending of money was a *mutuum*; hence any charge over and above restitution of the sum originally lent would be usury and so unacceptable morally and legally. This reflected no doubt the Aristotelian influence conceiving of money as barren.

An interesting side reflection here is that the Romans had not developed sensitivity to the macroeconomic phenomenon of inflation. In the context of the *mutuum* for lending of money one could imagine a compensation to lenders for the effects of inflation on the real purchasing power of the sum repaid by the borrower at the end of the loan period by analogy with the restoration of real capital intact in the event of a *commodatum*. Thus we could perhaps speak of an interest payment on a *mutuum* in such cases; or to put the point in terms of contemporary macroeconomics the borderline between interest and usurious extortion would not be at zero nominal rate of interest but rather at zero *real* rate; that is a nominal rate of interest equal to the rate of inflation over the period of the loan. We shall revert to this point later when treating some of the modern economic discussions of the questions of interest and usury. That being said the "interest" payment here described does not represent any gain to the lender but rather would be strictly speaking a payment to cover the damages incurred from the loss of purchasing power of the sums of money over the period of the loan due to inflation.

We cannot leave this discussion of the ancients without making reference to the Biblical pronouncements on the topic, pronouncements which were to affect profoundly mediaeval thinking and European history. The trouble is that the Bible yields a horribly mixed message on this whole question. On the one hand we have the Old Testament pronouncement of God to the Jewish people through the prophet Moses before entry to the Promised Land:

> Thou shalt not lend upon usury to thy brother; usury of money; usury of victuals; usury of anything that is lent upon usury. Unto a stranger thou mayest lend upon usury; but unto thy brother thou shalt not lend upon usury, that the Lord thy God may bless thee in all that thou settest thine hand to in the land whither thou goest to possess it.[10]

As Yaron Brook has so succinctly put it in his comprehensive article on the Morality of Moneylending:

> In one breath, God forbade usury outright; in another, He forbade the Jews to engage in usury with other Jews but permitted them to make loans at interest to non-Jews.[11]

On the other hand we have the New Testament where in the Christian Gospels the condemnation by Jesus Christ for whom any lending of money at interest to anyone is regarded as usurious robbery. It must be borne in mind that for a true Christian my brother is all mankind and there can be no question of making discriminatory distinctions of treatment between brothers, friends and acquaintances on the one hand and foreigners or enemies on the other; this is repeatedly emphasised in the Gospels, for example, in the Parable of the Good Samaritan[12]; while in the gospel of St Luke Christ unambiguously says:

> But love your enemies, and do good, and **lend, expecting nothing in return**, and your reward will be great, and you will be sons of the Most High, for he is kind to the ungrateful and the evil.[13]

The Bible as such thus portrays a horribly confused message that was to haunt Christianity itself and its relation with Judaism for centuries if not up to the present day. Broadly speaking the great Christian Fathers of the Church and in particular the great mediaeval philosopher St Thomas Aquinas argued very much along Aristotelian lines that any charging of interest on loans was usury and so sinful, morally unacceptable. At the same time the Jews had always held charging interest to fellow Jews to be morally dubious (even though many Jews still charge interest to other Jews), charging of interest to "gentiles", that is to non-Jews, was entirely fair game in the light of the Old Testament pronouncements on the subject. This position at once explains how the Jews became the predominant moneylenders of mediaeval Europe; and also why so much animosity developed with the Christians. For not only were the Jews the hated moneylenders demanding their pound of flesh at all costs, to good Christians they seemed to be acting in violation of the moral principles of loving all mankind and of the consequent prohibition of usury enunciated in the New Testament. Yaron Brook and others have documented how this animosity regularly boiled over into anti-Jewish pogroms in mediaeval Europe.[14]

As mentioned Aquinas and other Christian mediaeval thinkers who took over from Aristotle the framework of the philosophy of Natural Law argued primarily that all interest payment involved usurious extortion in the light of the natural barrenness of money argument that we found in Aristotle and which in strict economic terms may be quite defensible as we saw. But another distinct line of argument is also detectable and it foreshadows some of the arguments to be advanced in a contemporary context later in this book. This is what Walsh and Lynch label as the argument from compulsion.[15] In the context of the Middle Ages where economic growth was virtually zero in an agrarian society practically all loans other than those to finance wars for barons and princes were loans to unfortunate consumers who as a result of sickness, injury or plain bad luck at various times had not enough money to be able to feed, clothe and house themselves. Loans given to such unfortunates were typically given at very high rates of interest/usury and were entirely to finance consumption; there was no question whatever of the loans being converted into forms of real capital which could yield a productive return. Therefore to the mediaeval Schoolmen these loans seemed to be pure extortion whereby those who disposed of funds were profiting (and handsomely) from the misery and misfortune of others. In terms to be elaborated in much more detail later in the work such loans to the needy were made in a situation where there was huge power imbalance between the borrower and the lender, between debtor and creditor; and so like all extortion they involved an abusive power relationship very much akin to that which prevails in extortionate back street lending today.

Prohibition of interest in Islam

Perhaps for most people today when they hear of the prohibition of interest what comes to mind is Islamic finance rather than the arcane debates on the topic among the ancient Greeks and Romans or the mediaeval Schoolmen. Not only is this because there has been a fairly unambiguous prohibition of the taking of interest on loans in Islam from its earliest days, it is also because in the contemporary world systems of banking and finance which at least in principle operate without interest can be found in certain Islamic states and in certain Islamic banks worldwide. The doctrinal situation we shall find is quite similar to that of mediaeval Christianity and this is not surprising since both mediaeval Schoolmen and the great early Arab Muslim philosophers drew inspiration in philosophical matters from the works of Aristotle.

The prohibition of taking of interest on loans as being always usurious and so an ill-gotten gain could hardly be more clear than what is found in the Quran.

> Those who benefit from interest shall be raised like those who have been driven to madness by the touch of the Devil; this is because they say: "Trade is like interest" while God has permitted trade and forbidden interest … God deprives interest of all blessings but blesses charity. ... O believers, fear God, and give up the interest that remains outstanding if you are believers. If you do not do so, then be sure of being at war with God and His messenger. But, if you repent, you can have your principal.[16]

The Arabic word for interest on loans is an instance of the more general term *riba* which means an exchange in which what is exchanged is not equivalent, and so in effect one party is cheating or gaining at the expense of the other. Influenced by the Aristotelian notion of the essentially barren nature of money, any lending at interest involved an unfair exchange with the terms loaded in favour of the lender. There is however a very significant let-out in the Quranic position which seems to concede that certain types of exchange or trading need *not* be zero sum (whereas Aristotle had considered all chrematistic exchange for gain to be zero sum). The above verse clearly tells us that God has permitted trade but forbidden interest: thus in Islam the possibility of mutual gain from trade (non-zero sum game) is admitted and indeed fully permitted. What is forbidden is exchange where there is no such potential (for many games and business situations are indeed zero sum), and such exchanges are seen as exploitative. The charging of interest on loans is very clearly seen as an instance of such indefensible *riba*, of an unearned gain in an unfair exchange. For the reasons already outlined above when looking at Aristotle's position on the barrenness of money this argument is actually quite admissible. But if the lending is carried out to facilitate trade or investment which leads to the possibility of mutual gain in some non-zero-sum game, then in Islamic terms it is acceptable and equitable that the lender should participate in the gains or losses of the game. This distinction in effect between the barrenness of money per se and the potential productivity of real capital lies at the heart of contemporary approaches to Islamic finance; and we will argue in later chapters that it is both theoretically valid and a valuable pointer to a better form of finance.

The later Middle Ages in Europe

From the 13th century onwards the evolving economic realities in Europe brought in their train some significant developments in the moral evaluation of moneylending. This was the period when trade and commerce between Europe and Asia began to flourish, and the great trading merchants (the mercantile capitalists) had increasing need of trade credits of all kinds to finance their rapidly growing volume of especially international business. Indeed without credit lines it would have been very difficult to imagine how the extensive import of goods from Asia to Europe, which at the time necessitated long (typically 4–9 months) and hazardous sea voyages could have been financed. Hence economic realities began to force at least a re-appraisal of the arguments surrounding moneylending in Europe and it is from this time that the arguments about interest and usury begin to be cast in terms of their economic effects as well as purely in moral terms.

This was also the period when the great works of Aristotle and other Greek thinkers began to be rediscovered in Europe (ironically partly through contact with and translation of the great Arabic scholars of North Africa), and the Christian Church enthusiastically began to delve into the works of Aristotle in particular to refine and elaborate on Christian doctrine. Where early mediaeval thought had been dominated by the Bible and biblical exegesis later mediaeval thought comes to rely to a much greater extent on reasoning while not of course abandoning Biblical principles. Perhaps the greatest exponent of this dual approach drawing both on the Bible and on reason was St Thomas Aquinas (1225–1274). In terms of the moneylending debates this led to a new openness to rational discussion about the merits or demerits of the practice which was now cast not just in terms of Biblical injunctions and interpretations of these but also in terms of the real economic effects of moneylending practices which were becoming clear for all to see in the era of mercantile capitalism. Moneylending was making possible the transmission of the savings of the wealthy aristocratic class into investment in trade and commerce by the emergent merchant capitalists, thereby facilitating the flourishing economic growth that trade and commerce were bringing to those European cities and principalities involved.

In effect by the late Middle Ages moneylending at interest had become widespread in Europe and indeed it was not just the prerogative of Jewish moneylenders as in earlier centuries: Christian monks had become very predominant in the financing of trade and commerce on credits (they were in fact the early forerunners of many modern banks). Of course the practice was rather camouflaged by making the relevant extra charges in the guise of exchange rate commissions, overtly or covertly. Given the great proliferation of currencies at the time (each major principality having its own currency) it very often happened in the financing of international trade and commerce that a credit might be given in one currency only to be paid back in another; and it was in this money changing especially that the monks were heavily involved … and where they made their "commissions".[17]

So economic realities combined with a renewed willingness to engage in a rational debate led to some very significant developments in the whole moral appraisal of moneylending; and it is from this time that the more purely economic arguments began to play a significant role in the debate. The first obvious impact of this was the distinction to which already some reference has been made at the beginning of this chapter between *interest* and *usury*. From the early 13th century[18] it was explicitly held that while usury in the sense of asking back more than what was lent at the termination of a loan could not be tolerated, it would be permissible to make a charge for any damages that may have occurred to the object lent and this latter was called *interest* rather than usury. The application of interest in the case of a physical object or piece of equipment lent (real capital goods) is straightforward and is in effect a compensation for depreciation of the equipment; but in the case of money it is of course difficult to see how there can be any depreciation other than what occurs through the effects of macroeconomic price inflation (or its very prevalent first cousin in those days, debasement of the coinage). So while owners of real capital equipment could charge interest as in the ancient Roman *commodatum* loan[19] the charging of interest on loans of money was still regarded as usurious and immoral. Some mediaeval thinkers sought to extend the notion of compensation for loss to the very modern idea of opportunity cost to the lender both in terms of alternative investment opportunities foregone or of simple time preference (foregoing consumption today for consumption tomorrow in the event of lending) but the major Church thinkers such as St Thomas Aquinas as well as a succession of general Councils of the Church in the 14th century rejected these extensions of the interest argument. Time it was held belongs to God and not to man and therefore it is not for man to charge to another man simply for time, for deferred consumption. So officially moneylending at interest remained in principle usurious and if Christians were to become involved with profitable moneylending it would have to take the form of money-changing or even more complex ruses like the triple contract.[20] This latter is decidedly scholastic but nonetheless interesting since for the first time the idea that a compensation for taking risk may be a justification for making an extra charge when loans are repaid clearly emerges. The triple contract can only be applied to a business venture since to be put in place there must be some potential for the money lent to generate new profits (as with the loans to mercantile capitalists to finance their trading). The lender enters a partnership with the borrower; there is a second agreement to share in the profits or losses of the venture; and then there is a third contract whereby the lender accepts a lesser certain repayment (i.e. repayment of an interest bearing loan, *debt* financing in effect) *instead of* a notionally greater but uncertain repayment which would share out the profits of the venture between borrower and lender, *equity* financing in effect). This triple contract arrangement as we shall see later foreshadows some of the key debates and instruments of contemporary Islamic finance and indeed of the wider debate on the political economy of the charging of interest on loans which is central to this work.

By the end of the mediaeval period the whole question of the morality of the charging of interest on loans, of moneylending, banking and the financing of trade and commerce had at once become much more nuanced and ambiguous (like many other issues in the late mediaeval Church such as indulgences); and the debate as we have seen had begun to move away from mere biblical exegesis to a serious consideration of the economic effects of the practices of moneylending. With the Reformation of the 16th century and then the Enlightenment (17th century onwards) and the Industrial Revolution (late 18th century) the whole debate was to be transformed into predominantly an economic appraisal of the effects of moneylending in terms of *efficiency* although vestiges of the old moral argument remained in the guise of appraisal of the *equity* effects of moneylending.[21] That evolving post-Reformation debate we shall examine in the next chapter.

Notes

1 Speech of José Mujica to G20 Conference, 20 June 2012 in Rio de Janeiro, available at https://thewanderlife.com/human-happiness-and-the-environment-address-by-uruguayan-president-jose-mujica-at-rio-20-summit/ accessed 29 April 2024.

2 It is by definition difficult to pin down exact data on interest rates for back street lending but some data are available for payday loans. The following warning may be found on an independent financial advice website in UK: "Payday loans must usually be repaid over anything from a couple of days to a month; the typical cost of borrowing £300 would usually be about £75 — equivalent to roughly 1,300 per cent" available at http://www.thisismoney.co.uk/money/cardsloans/article-2026725/Thousands-middle-income-earners-turn-backstreet-payday-loans.html#ixzz3ouceN9la accessed 12 July 2024.

3 There is some evidence that the taking of interest, especially of excessive interest was frowned upon in ancient Hindu and Buddhist thought, long before the Greeks began to reflect thereon. See for example: Visser, W., & McIntosh, A. (1998). A Short History of the Historical Critique of Usury. *Accounting, Business and Financial History* 8(2):175–189.

4 ARISTOTLE (1969). *Nicomachean Ethics*. Translated by Ross, D. Oxford: Oxford University Press. ARISTOTLE (1995). *The Politics of Aristotle*. Translated by Baker, E. Oxford: Oxford University Press.

5 The unquestioned purity and optimism of this view of the world is striking: there is no room in the Greek vision for evil as in Judaeo-Christian thought or as in the Yin and Yang of Chinese thought.

6 See Sartre, J.-P. (1973). *Existentialism and Humanism*. London: Methuen, *passim*.

7 ARISTOTLE (1995). *The Politics of Aristotle*. Translated by Baker, E. Oxford: University Press Oxford. Book 1, chapter 10

8 Walsh, A., & Lynch, T. (2015). *The Morality of Money*. London: Palgrave Macmillan. See p. 95.

9 See Walsh, A., & Lynch, T. (2015). *The Morality of Money*. London: Palgrave Macmillan, p. 96.

10 Deuteronomy 23:19–20. available at Bible Gateway https://www.biblegateway.com/passage/?search=Deuteronomy%2023%3A19-20&version=ESV accessed 29 October 2024.

11 See: Brook, Y. (2007). The Morality of Moneylending: A Short History. *The Objective Standard* 2(3 Fall 2007). Available online at https://www.theobjectivestandard.com/issues/2007-fall/morality-of-moneylending/ accessed 12 July 2024.

12 The Parable of the Good Samaritan can be found in the Gospel of St Luke 10:25–37. It is also worth quoting the Gospel of St Matthew on this point to show how unambiguous is the Christian position: "*You have heard that it was said, 'Love your neighbour[a] and hate your enemy'. 44 But I tell you, love your enemies and pray for those who persecute you, 45 that you may be children of your Father in heaven. He causes his sun to rise on the evil and the good, and sends rain on the righteous and the unrighteous. 46 If you love those who love you, what reward will you get? Are not even the tax collectors doing that? 47 And if you greet only your own people, what are you doing more than others? Do not even pagans do that? 48 Be perfect, therefore, as your heavenly Father is perfect*". Matthew 5:43–48. Both passages available at https://www.biblegateway.com accessed 12 July 2024.

13 Gospel of St Luke 6:35 (bold emphasis ours) available at Bible Gateway op.cit. https://www.biblegateway.com/passage/?search=+Luke+6+%3A35+&version=NIV accessed 12 July 2024.

14 See Brook, Y. (2007). The Morality of Moneylending: A Short History. *The Objective Standard* 2(3 Fall 2007). Available online at https://www.theobjectivestandard.com/issues/2007-fall/morality-of-moneylending/ accessed 12 July 2024.

15 Walsh, A., & Lynch, T. (2015). *The Morality of Money*. London: Palgrave Macmillan, pp. 96–97.

16 Quran 2:275–280, available at https://legacy.quran.com/2/275–281 accessed 12 July 2024.

17 On this point and on the emergence of banking in late mediaeval Europe in general, see De Roover, R. (2008). *Money Banking and Credit in Mediaeval Bruges: Italian Merchant Bankers, Lombards and Money Changers*. London: Read Books.

18 See Brook, Y. (2007). The Morality of Moneylending: A Short History. *The Objective Standard* 2(3 Fall 2007). Available online at https://www.theobjectivestandard.com/issues/2007-fall/morality-of-moneylending/ accessed 12 July 2024.

19 See above pg 12.

20 See Walsh, A., & Lynch, T. (2015). *The Morality of Money*. London: Palgrave Macmillan, pp. 98–99.

21 In contemporary normative Political Economy (also known as welfare economics), the normative appraisal of the performance of the economy is said to be based both on the criterion of *efficiency* of resource allocation and on the criterion of *equity* of distribution of wealth and opportunities.

Bibliography

ARISTOTLE (1969). *Nicomachean Ethics*, translated by Ross, D. Oxford: University Press Oxford.

ARISTOTLE (1995). *The Politics of Aristotle*, translated by Baker, E. Oxford: University Press Oxford.

Bible Gateway website, available https://www.biblegateway.com accessed 12 July 2024.

Brook, Y. (2007). The Morality of Moneylending: A Short History. *The Objective Standard* 2(3 Fall 2007). Available online at https://www.theobjectivestandard.com/issues/2007-fall/morality-of-moneylending/ accessed 12 July 2024.

De Roover, R. (2008). *Money Banking and Credit in Mediaeval Bruges: Italian Merchant Bankers, Lombards and Money Changers*. London: Read Books.

Mujica, J. (2012). *Speech to G20 Conference* 20 June 2012 in Rio de Janeiro, available at https://thewanderlife.com/human-happiness-and-the-environment-address-by-uruguayan-president-jose-mujica-at-rio-20-summit/ accessed 29 April 2024.

Quran website, available at https://legacy.quran.com/2/275-281 accessed 12 July 2024.

Sartre, J.-P. (1973). *Existentialism and Humanism*. London: Methuen.

Thisismoney.co.uk (financial website). Available at https://www.thisismoney.co.uk/money/cardsloans/article-2026725/Thousands-middle-income-earners-turn-back-street-payday-loans.html#ixzz3ouceN9la accessed 12 July 2024.

Visser, W., & McIntosh, A. (1998). A Short History of the Historical Critique of Usury. *Accounting, Business and Financial History* 8(2):175–189.

Walsh, A., & Lynch, T. (2015). *The Morality of Money*. London: Palgrave Macmillan.

3 Transition of the moral debate to political economy

From Bacon to the contemporary discussions of interest and usury

As we saw at the end of the last chapter the incessant moral debate about the morality of usury and the charging of interest on loans began from the late Middle Ages to focus to a greater extent on the micro and macroeconomic effects of moneylending rather than on the pure micro morality of the act of lending at interest, and this in turn was a reflection of the evolving reality of mercantile capitalism and its burgeoning trade financing needs. With the moral watershed that was the Protestant Reformation and later the Enlightenment and its eventual fruits in the Industrial Revolution of the 18th century the debate was to be almost entirely transformed into a discussion of the economic effects of the practice of moneylending at interest. In this chapter we trace that evolution and we will argue that while there was a growing consensus especially among economists on the economic beneficence of the practice insofar as it facilitated economic growth through the transmission of loanable funds (savings) into business investment, the arguments are not as clear-cut as might superficially seem to be the case. We shall also argue that the purely moral question has not entirely gone away even if conveniently overlooked by most contemporary commentators; it is present in the recurrent concerns over extortion and equity in relation to certain types of racketeer moneylending

Protestantism and moneylending

The Protestant Reformation spearheaded by Martin Luther and John Calvin certainly brought a fresh approach to the whole usury debate as conducted in the16th century. Luther recognised the undoubted facilitation of trade and commerce which moneylending brought, and given the economic benefits of such merchant capitalism in terms of growth and feeding the people, he regarded the practice as inevitable. Curiously however he still regarded the practice of charging interest as inherently immoral and inconsistent with the Christian principle of loving one's neighbour as oneself but its inevitability as a practice was put down to humans' imperfection arising from Original Sin.[1] Hence he could accept the practice as inevitable but argued that the

DOI: 10.4324/9781003546030-3

rates and circumstances of charging of interest should be strictly regulated by the state. Calvin went much further than Luther and can be seen as the first Christian thinker to argue that the taking of interest was not in itself immoral. He rejected the Aristotelian argument of the inequity of interest based on the barrenness of money argument,[2] because contemporary mercantile trade and commerce had patently shown that a stream of returns could be generated by the borrower in which it seemed entirely fair that the lender should have a stake. Calvin who was at pains to bring Christianity back to the purity of the simple Biblical message after the centuries of ever more decadent exegesis of the sacred texts by the Scholastics argued moreover that since in the Old Testament Jews had been explicitly permitted by God to lend at interest to Gentiles (non-Jews) while being prohibited from lending at interest to fellow Jews that the practice of lending at interest was not after all inherently sinful. Consistently with the universality of the Christian message Calvin therefore held that anybody could lend to anyone at interest, but he also held that where the lending becomes exploitative (as in the case of lending at interest to poor people in times of hardship), this would still be considered to be immoral.

The thoughts of these and other Protestant reformers inspired in part by a simple observation of the practical utility and productivity of mercantile moneylending form a kind of transition to the more purely economic arguments devoid of any moral or religious dimension that were to come to dominate the moneylending debates in Europe from the Enlightenment onwards. In effect just like in our own day as new technologies become established and utilised, certain practices which previously might have raised ethical concerns become normalised (genetic engineering, in vitro fertilisation), so also as the charging of interest became a widespread commercial practice especially as merchant trading and commerce between Europe and the Far East became pervasive, it came to be an accepted practice albeit with a residual of reservations, and the ethical concerns of earlier ages receded.

The enlightenment and the early economists

With the Enlightenment and the flourishing of a strictly rational approach to apprehension and understanding of at least the material universe, the arguments about moneylending at interest thus came to be almost entirely grounded in concrete economic realities. Thinkers such as the great English experimental scientist Francis Bacon writing in the early 17th century openly argued that lending of money to businesses is patently capable of generating returns over and above the sum lent, that money is therefore productive and not barren and so that it is not inequitable that in such cases the lender should ask for a return over and above the sum lent. For Bacon this was an argument of simple economics. Nonetheless as a kind of afterthought, like Luther and Calvin, Bacon feared that in certain cases the charging of interest could become exploitative, and therefore he held that a strict state regulation of the rates chargeable should be in place.

By the late 18th and early 19th century with the Industrial Revolution in full swing and the emergence of Economics (or of Political Economy as it was then typically called) as a distinct and rigorous discipline, the discussions about moneylending and interest became the almost exclusive domain of economists who studied the phenomena in an empirically grounded manner based on observation of the workings of actual economic systems. Indeed in its early days (if not right up to the present day in the case of neoclassical economics) economists sought explicitly to break away from philosophical speculation and to model their methods on the rigorous experimental approach of Physics, Chemistry and other natural sciences which had yielded such huge advances in natural science over the centuries since the time of Francis Bacon. In this perspective the concerns of the ancient and scholastic thinkers seemed abstruse and irrelevant and the concern was to examine how the economic system as a whole (macroeconomics) and in its parts (microeconomics) actually worked (in those times). In carrying out this project economists simply accepted that moneylending at interest exists and they sought to analyse the central role which it appeared in practice to play in the system. To early economists like Adam Smith the payment of interest was an inevitable aspect of the allocation of the loanable funds of wealthy savers to risky investments and the justification if such was needed was utilitarian; in the end the practice is beneficial insofar as it facilitates and promotes productive investment and so economic growth and prosperity for all in the society. The great founder of Utilitarianism as a moral philosophy, Jeremy Bentham, similarly saw no need to provide any other justification of the charging of interest than the utilitarian argument that it promotes productive investment and so economic growth, and he was explicitly dismissive of the Aristotelian argument that money is barren. Later in the 19th century Nassau Senior and, the great Cambridge economist, Alfred Marshall while not wishing to get embroiled in the arcane ethical debates added the argument that interest on loans can be considered a reward for abstinence from current consumption or as a reward for waiting. The great Austrian economist of capital theory, Böhm-Bawerk also saw interest in terms of time preference (immediate consumption preferred to deferred consumption), but he also introduced the notion that "roundabout" methods of production whereby when money is used to invest in capital equipment and it subsequently increases the output of simple immediate production by labour, then that use of money is productive of new or greater value and so deserves a reward in the form of interest on the monies lent for investment.[3] Despite seeking to analyse the phenomena in purely factual terms it may be noted that in particular in the later 19th- and early 20th-century economists there is a whiff of moral argument still detectable: somehow the argument is being made that the lender *deserves* a reward for his/her abstinence or waiting, deserving being clearly a term of moral approbation.

Contemporary economics: a summary of the arguments

At this point rather than going into the detail of the pronouncements of ranges of the many economists who have dealt with the theme, it may be more useful to attempt a summary of the typical arguments which are proffered by contemporary economists on the role and functions of moneylending at interest in the world economy today. One reason for taking this approach is that a sort of weary consensus has taken root in contemporary mainstream Economics on these questions and brief reference to it can readily be found in a wide variety of textbooks and the like.[4] The arguments either by way of explanation or justification of moneylending at interest can we believe be summarised as follows:

1 The argument as to *productivity* of money. When money is lent to a business for purposes of investment in real capital of various kinds (equipment, real estate or even human capital in the form of education of the workforce) the business will, at least if the investment is successful and profitable, yield a flow of returns to the investor from which it will be possible to make an interest payment without extortion to the lender. It is typically held that money is therefore not barren but productive and that the lender therefore somehow deserves to share in this profit flow arising from the productive use of the money lent; the lender deserves to receive an interest payment on the loan. In effect what is suggested by this line of argumentation is that while sums of money may have many possible uses, when they are lent to a productive enterprise they allow the enterprise to purchase equipment (or invest in the human capital of employees) which in turn will increase the productivity of the company. In short money is being considered to be somehow a generic factor of production whereas labour, land or real capital equipment are considered to be factors specific to specific production processes. But insofar as it is a factor of production as such it deserves or it is somehow natural that like labour or land it should be entitled to a fixed reward defined in advance; and that reward is fixed interest.
2 The argument of *opportunity cost*. In Economics the opportunity cost of any activity is defined as the value of the next best opportunity foregone by being involved in that activity. When a scarce resource is committed to any particular use, precisely because of that scarcity, some alternative uses of the resource are foregone and the value of these is the opportunity cost. This is in fact the precise definition of cost for economists. Now in the case of moneylending one might challenge the implicit idea in the productivity argument (argument 1 above) that the lender deserves a fixed reward from the profit stream of the investment which the lending made possible: why should the lender get a share since in effect they have not put in any concrete effort? The money lent had to be converted into one of the primary

factors of production (human capital, capital equipment, land or concrete knowledge) before any real contribution to output could result from the money. One answer to this type of (Aristotelian) question could be the opportunity cost argument which holds that when money is lent out lenders forego the opportunity of using that money for themselves in alternative direct productive investments which could yield them profits. Therefore they deserve to be rewarded for this opportunity foregone. Moneylending has a (opportunity) cost and the payment of interest on loans covers this cost.

We may also note a perhaps more problematic variant of the opportunity cost argument which focuses on the sacrifice of current consumption possibilities by the lender, the so-called *abstinence* or *waiting* argument (traceable back to Nassau Senior and Marshall's thinking in the 19th century as outlined above). Here it is noted that in lending out funds the lender is foregoing the possibility of using those funds immediately for current consumption activities; lenders abstain from current consumption and are foregoing the possibility of indulging themselves immediately against the possibility of (perhaps) indulging themselves at a later date. This abstinence is seen as a "suffering" and so as an opportunity cost that therefore deserves to be offset by the payment of interest by the borrower. In the *waiting* variant of this argument it is not so much abstinence that is emphasised as the fact that when the money is lent out which is almost invariably for an agreed period of time; if the lender should in the interim have need of the funds because of unforeseen emergencies requiring immediate spending (or injection of liquidity in the case of institutional lenders), the funds lent out will simply not be available. This "illiquidity" is once again a "suffering" and so an opportunity cost incurred by the lender and it deserves to be offset by the payment of interest.

It should be noted however that especially in the abstinence argument it is implicitly recognised that among the alternative uses of loanable funds in addition to lending for purposes of business investment, there is also the possibility of using the funds purely for current consumption. We will revert to the significance of this point later in this book.

3 Once we begin to explain or justify interest in terms of (opportunity) costs for the lender we encounter another very commonly proffered argument; the argument of *compensation for risks* taken by the lender. In this argument the key reason for charging interest is that the business investments or other uses to which the loan is put by the borrower may or may not in the end yield a stream of profitable returns and in worst case scenarios much or even all of the money may be lost and the lender will have to write off the loan. This risk certainly exists and in reality is quite significant in many sectors of activity (i.e. it is not just hypothetical), and it is said to give rise to or to justify the payment of interest for two slightly different reasons. The first reason is that the lender suffers anxiety and stress at the thought that there is a risk of the loan not being paid back in full and

that this stress deserves to be compensated (a variant of the risk aversion argument commonly found among economists and pervasive in finance theory). The stress at the thought of risk is in effect a cost or suffering of the lender that deserves to be compensated by interest. The second reason that is offered is in terms of portfolio management effects, an argument which would be particularly relevant to justify the charging of interest by large institutional lenders. In any large portfolio of loans there is inevitably the risk that some of the loans will "not perform", that is to say that the borrower will default in part or in full. Therefore by charging interest on all loans an institutional investor can guarantee that over the whole portfolio no losses are incurred. In effect this is an *insurance against risk* type of argument to defend the charging of interest. The question of whether the interest charges should be just sufficient to guarantee the repayment of the sum total of principals over the whole portfolio or if they should yield a net gain over the whole portfolio to the lenders over and above the sum total of the principals is left open on this variant of the risk compensation argument.

4 It is also worth noting here the so-called *agio* or *time preference* argument which is really a first cousin of the abstinence argument reviewed earlier (in argument 2 above, opportunity cost). It is held that for an amalgam of reasons human beings prefer immediate current consumption to future consumption of goods and services. Partly this is because of immediacy as in the abstinence theory (*carpe diem*); partly it is because of uncertainty regarding the future as in the risk argument. But now the risk is focussed on the risks of deferring consumption of one's wealth rather than that the loan may not perform. If we defer consumption then at a later date when the loan is repaid the world may have changed in manifold ways, the same goods may not be readily available and of course, we as lenders may have changed and, horror of horrors, we could even be dead![5] For all of these reasons the *agio* theorists hold that people have a time preference in favour of the present and so once again when lending occurs the lender is going against this innate time preference, "suffers" or incurs a cost thereby and so deserves to be compensated by the payment of interest.

5 A rather different line of argument emphasises that the vast bulk of lending occurs through the medium of financial intermediation: through banks of all kinds (commercial and investment) and through various types of hedge funds etc. These are large scale institutional lenders whose professional activity is financial intermediation: passing on funds from savers to eventual borrowers in a manner that renders a real service to savers. Running such financial intermediation "firms" requires skilled labour and high-quality equipment, and the costs of the financial firms thus need to be covered. The charging of interest can then be justified as being at least one way in which these relatively fixed costs of a banking business can be covered. However apart from the fact that this linkage is at best approximate in its relation to the costs of a financial intermediation business

it has to be recognised that in today's world digital technologies of various kinds allied with the internet and artificial intelligence (AI) have rendered the costs of intermediation considerably lower without any marked permanent drop in interest rates (which reflect rather the macroeconomic stance of central bank monetary policies, rates of inflation expected etc. rather than intermediation costs). Crowdfunding puts ultimate borrowers in direct contact with savers without any intermediation; while AI applications and algorithms are increasingly used for example in assessments of creditworthiness.

6 Each of the foregoing five arguments is microeconomic in focus insofar as they concentrate on the economics and ethics of the individual act of lending whether by an individual or by an institution. It is also possible to give an economic explanation or moral justification of the charging of interest on loans in macroeconomic terms; that is to say that interest is explained and justified in terms of the impact of the practice on the financial system and on the whole of the economy. The most basic argument in this vein to be found in all classical and neoclassical economists as well as in all contemporary textbooks is that financial institutions of all kinds (retail banks, investment banks, hedge funds of various kinds) are involved in *financial intermediation*, that is the transmission of loanable funds in the hands of ultimate savers (individual or corporate) to the hands of ultimate borrowers usually conceived of as businesses wishing to invest in new ventures or equipment (although the ultimate borrowers could also of course be consumers given the scale of consumer borrowing today).[6] In this financial intermediation process interest is said to play a central role as in some vaguely defined sense a *price for money lent*; as a key variable which allows the market for loanable funds to balance demand and supply through a pricing mechanism and thus to clear itself on an on-going basis as any other market. Interest in short is a price with a key market clearing role in the whole macroeconomic process of financial intermediation.

7 A further macroeconomic argument which is sometimes encountered (mainly in macroeconomic or monetary theory textbooks) is that as things stand today the *control of interest rates* is also a *central tool of macroeconomic monetary policy*. In a purely factual sense this is indeed correct. Monetary policy is both expressed in terms of[7] and conducted in practice through manipulation of interest rates by central banks, and financial markets are hugely influenced by these manipulations both directly and indirectly through the impact which rate manipulations have on money supply and liquidity and on expectations of inflation and economic growth in the markets. As John Sloman put it in his textbook:

> The approach to monetary control today in many countries is to focus directly on interest rates ... most governments or central banks have used interest rate changes as the major means of keeping aggregate demand and inflation under control.[8]

It will be clear from the above summary of contemporary arguments regarding lending at interest that there is a widely shared consensus to the effect that the payment of interest on loans is not only an inevitable and even indispensable feature of a contemporary economic system but also fully justifiable. It is true that the contemporary argument is almost entirely cast in terms of the micro and macroeconomic roles of interest although at micro level as we saw there is a recurrent tendency not only to explain but somehow also to *justify morally* the payment of interest, for example as a reward for abstinence or for risk-taking. In view of the huge body of overhanging mediaeval literature and argument against the charging of interest or at least of usurious interest on loans (as seen in earlier chapters of this work), one may wonder if this has been completely overthrown or if it has left any traces in today's world. Actually despite the prevailing economic consensus favourable to moneylending at interest one can find occasional pockets of moral disquiet relating to cases of what are seen as extortionate lending. Of course this is not new having been a recurrent theme ever since Francis Bacon[9] began to evolve the modern arguments broadly favourable to interest on loans, but it does provide us with an insight into the sort of circumstances in which even to the contemporary realistic or even jaundiced mind certain practices in respect of charging interest can seem to be abusive and so morally unacceptable. Fundamentally many commentators recognise that in circumstances where the power relationship between lender and borrower is severely skewed with the lender in a position to impose severe or draconian conditions of repayment on the borrower, such lending can be deemed to be an abuse of power and so inequitable; extortion in effect. That such lending exists to this day let there be no mistake: it is present in the phenomenon of payday loans (short-term credit to low-wage earners to tide them over until future receipt of wages and payable on payday), and it is also present in the necessarily more hidden practices of back street loan sharks that thrive in marginalised neighbourhoods of big cities around the world often involving illegal immigrants. The interest on such loans is typically astronomical when converted to equivalent annual percentage rate (APR); in a number of recent reports on the phenomenon of payday loans in the UK, for example, loans of £100 with required repayment at the end of one month of £125 have been reported as quite common; this is the equivalent of an APR compound interest rate of 1,455% (or of 400% if only simple interest were applied, but this latter is rarely the case; interest charged monthly is compounded monthly).[10] These practices are frowned upon by most, regarded as deeply immoral by many others; and in many countries they are also illegal (under usury laws which still survive in the guise of maximum legally enforceable interest rates). It would not therefore be inaccurate to say that as a footnote to the prevailing consensus favourable to moneylending at interest there is also present an abiding aversion to the charging of "excessive" interest in situations where there is a skewed power relationship between lender and borrower which allows the lender to take an unfair advantage and to extort the borrower.

We shall return to this theme in a later chapter since it reveals, we believe, a central point in the whole moral argument over the charging of interest on loans: moral disquiet not so much about the payment of interest per se seen as a kind of theft (as in the Aristotelian barrenness argument) but rather as involving somehow an abuse of power and so an inequitable treatment of man by man.

Notes

1 Luther, M. (1524). *On Commerce and Usury*. Edited by Rössner, P. London: Anthem Press, p. 125.
2 See Walsh, A., & Lynch, T. (2015). *The Morality of Money*. London: Palgrave Macmillan, p. 102.
3 Böhm Bawerk actually devoted a whole treatise to the subject, and it is regarded as a *locus classicus* of Austrian Economics; see: Böhm-Bawerk, E. (1890). *Capital and Interest*. London: Macmillan.
4 For a succinct summary of the various theories, see Lipsey, R., & Chrystal, A. (2011). *Economics*, 12th ed., Oxford: Oxford University Press, chapter 12; or Sloman, J., Garratt, D, & Guest, J. (2022). *Economics*, 11th ed., Harlow: Pearson Prentice Hall, chapter 22. There are also various websites propounding theories of interest rates, but what is striking about these is the diversity of theories as seen by various contemporary economists and one might even say confusion regarding the topic. See for example Top 7 theories of interest with discussion https://www.economicsdiscussion.net/theories-of-interest/top-7-theories-of-interest-with-criticisms/21070 accessed 2 August 2023. Available at Bible Gateway https://www.biblegateway.com/passage/?search=Deuteronomy%2023%3A19-20&version=ESV accessed 29 October 2024.
5 One cannot but be reminded of the German philosopher Martin Heidegger's work in which a central theme is the recognition that "Man is a being towards death" or in German "*Sein zum Tode*". To live authentically human beings, live or should live their lives in a manner which frankly and systematically confronts their own mortality. See Heidegger, M. (1962). *Being and Time*. Translated from the German original by Macquarrie, J., & Robinson, E. Oxford: Basil Blackwell.
6 The typical form of this financial intermediation argument to explain the key macroeconomic role of the banking system and of other financial intermediaries by a peculiar sleight of hand usually obscures this presence of extensive consumer borrowing for consumption as opposed to business borrowing for investment in the contemporary economies of the advanced world. In aggregative macroeconomic analysis the Savings aggregate is defined in terms of that part of disposable income which is not spent on consumption. In this approach those loanable funds which get lent on to consumers actually cancel out and disappear from view in the macroeconomic Savings aggregate since consumers who are net borrowers (i.e. who spend *more* than their disposable income) are considered as *dis-savers* or negative savers and so their borrowing is subtracted out from the macroeconomics Savings aggregate measure. For purposes of certain basic types of aggregative macroeconomic analysis this may be a defensible analytical approach but it should be clear that an important part of the overall picture of the role and destination of loanable funds is being obscured by the abstraction.
7 Perhaps the clearest example of this central role of interest rates in relation to monetary policy is the Taylor rule (and variants thereof) which is widely used by central banks around the world as a basis for monetary policy. Although linked with the

attainment of an inflation target as ultimate goal (of monetary policy), the Taylor rule involves the explicit setting of interest rates with a view to attaining the inflation target. See, for example, Sloman, J., et al. (2022). *Economics*, 11th ed. Harlow: Pearson Prentice Hall, chapter 22.

8 Sloman, J., Garratt, D, & Guest, J. (2022). *Economics*, 11th ed. Harlow: Pearson Prentice Hall, p. 721.

9 See above pg 22.

10 On payday loans in general see Packman, C. (2012). *Loan Sharks: The Rise and Rise of Payday Lending*. London: Searching Finance; or on their consequences in practice Perry, S. (2011). *When Payday Loans Go Wrong*. London: Pneuma Springs. For detail of current practices and rates, see http://www.thisismoney.co.uk/money/cardsloans/article-2026725/Thousands-middle-income-earners-turn-backstreet-payday-loans.html#ixzz3ouceN9la accessed 12 July 2024. For compound interest tables see https://staff.emu.edu.tr/elnazgholipour/Documents/courses/ieng420/lecture-notes/spring-2020–2021/Interest-Tables.pdf accessed 12 July 2024.

Bibliography

Böhm-Bawerk, E. (1890). *Capital and Interest*. London: Macmillan.

Heidegger, M. (1962). *Being and Time*, translated from the German original by Macquarrie, J., & Robinson, E. Oxford: Basil Blackwell.

Lipsey, R., & Chrystal, A. (2011). *Economics*, 12th ed. Oxford: Oxford University Press.

Luther, M. (1524). *On Commerce and Usury*, edited by Rössner, P. London: Anthem Press.

Packman, C. (2012). *Loan Sharks: The Rise and Rise of Payday Lending*. London: Searching Finance.

Perry, S. (2011). *When Payday Loans Go Wrong*. London: Pneuma Springs.

Sloman, J., Garratt, D., & Guest, J. (2022). *Economics*, 11th ed. Harlow: Pearson Prentice Hall.

This is Money website, available at https://www.thisismoney.co.uk/money/cardsloans/article-2026725/Thousands-middle-income-earners-turn-backstreet-payday-loans.html#ixzz3ouceN9la accessed 12 July 2024.

Top 7 theories of interest with discussion https://www.economicsdiscussion.net/theories-of-interest/top-7-theories-of-interest-with-criticisms/21070 accessed 15 July 2024.

Walsh, A., & Lynch, T. (2015). *The Morality of Money*. London: Palgrave Macmillan.

4 A critical philosophico-economic appraisal of the contemporary consensus on moneylending at interest

The previous chapter has outlined a summary of the contemporary consensus on the arguments surrounding the charging of interest on loans and we have seen that it is a consensus that both see the practice as economically inevitable and is almost entirely in favour of it. There were only some peripheral moral reservations regarding cases of what could be deemed to be extortionate lending to be found as footnotes to this prevailing consensus. In this chapter we will however outline a systematic critique of that contemporary consensus seeking to show that it harbours serious contradictions at the level of purely economic argument and remains dubious if not eminently challengeable at the moral philosophical level. We would not claim originality for all of the arguments advanced here, and readers will detect clear echoes of some of the ancient and modern debates on usury. But what is perhaps unusual is to place the critique of the economic arguments directly alongside the moral philosophical critique and indeed to show how these two critiques are intertwined even in the most apparently hard-core economic arguments.

It will be useful to clarify here at the outset of this chapter certain presuppositions of the moral philosophical critique to be carried out. We will presume that the financial sector in general and financial intermediaries in particular are not to be considered as purely self-serving entities existing in isolation but rather that they are located in human societies and communities and so it can be expected that somehow they should contribute to the well-being or the smooth functioning of the communities in which they are located and which they serve. This is the most basic meaning of the term corporate social responsibility as elaborated in the literature and thinking of contemporary business ethics. It will also be presumed that the crude Friedmanite position according to which the "social responsibility of a business is to increase profits"[1] is neither automatic nor self-evident. That is to say that if financial firms and intermediaries of all kinds behave in a manner to maximise their profits or financial returns we cannot take it as automatically given that that will promote maximum well-being in the societies where those firms operate. We retain an open mind on that question; it may or may not be the case that profit maximising financial firms are promoting by their activities

DOI: 10.4324/9781003546030-4

a maximum of well-being; the case for a deregulated purely profit-oriented financial sector needs to be made rather than simply assumed and it may be that while some financial intermediation practices contribute handsomely to societal well-being, perhaps some others do not.

The contemporary consensus: a critical appraisal

We now review critically each element of the contemporary consensus which we identified in the last chapter.

1 The first argument for the payment of interest on loans which we encountered was that when money is lent to a business it can be turned into various types of real capital which can generate a stream of profit returns for the business and interest is the reward to the lender for this contribution to **productivity** achieved by the business. This productivity arises from what Böhm-Bawerk described as roundabout methods of production.[2] But to the critically acute mind as an argument specifically for payment of interest there is a sleight of hand present in this productivity argument. Money per se is *not* capital; it is not per se capable of generating a productive surplus. It is only when it is converted into a form of real capital that a productive surplus can be generated. After all, as mentioned before, any sum of money possessed by a lender could equally be used by said lender for a binge of pure consumption activity that would generate no productive surplus or profit flow of any kind. So Aristotle and the scholastics were not actually wrong when they said that money per se is barren: it is indeed so and may only become productive when it has been transformed into a form of real capital, a transformation which obviously is not automatic since sums of money are also regularly used for consumption purposes.

   If we concede that money per se is not productive but becomes so only when transformed into a form of real capital used in a productive enterprise, it is no longer automatic that money lent should earn a return in virtue of its productivity. Strictly speaking we would have to say that money should earn a return only when it is lent to a productive enterprise. But at this point an interesting mutation of the apparently purely economic argument from productivity is creeping into the picture; for when we begin to think in this way about the question of return to capital lent we are in effect getting into the broader issue of returns in the context of a business enterprise; in effect into the essentially *moral* question of entitlement to returns. It is said for example that the owner of the funds which are transformed into real capital somehow *deserves* a return in view of the productivity which the loan has unleashed. It must be emphasised that this question of entitlement to returns in a business enterprise has historically been the subject of heated debate in moral and social philosophy and in political economy. Karl Marx and other radical socialist thinkers have considered the return to the owner of capital to be an exploitation of the workforce, an unjust appropriation of the (surplus) value created by the workforce.[3] Without wishing to go to the perhaps implausible extremes of Marx's labour theory of value we can certainly question however the validity of the argument according to which the owner of funds deserves or is morally entitled to a return in the form of interest for the productivity that the injection of funds has made possible. At most the owner of funds can in justice be said to be entitled to a share in the eventual profits and losses of the business enterprise. In short where lent funds are used productively and generate profits they ground a moral case for the owners of funds to share in the profits and losses of the productive enterprises in question. Incidentally it might be objected on purely economic grounds of incentives and rewards that if a return in the form of fixed interest is not given the funds will not be lent. This is patently not the case as equity participation in businesses occurs extensively in conventional Western financing systems as well as being the norm in Islamic financing of businesses.[4] If at this point it were said that in effect we are transforming lenders into a type of passive or inactive entrepreneurs, we would say yes indeed that is the case. We are envisaging their role as in the *Mudarabah* arrangement of Islamic finance in effect. (As we will see in Chapter 5, in *Mudarabah* the lenders/investors are not in any way involved in the everyday management of the business and in that sense they are passive participants; but they will be rewarded on the basis of the profits or losses realised in proportions of these that are determined at the outset in the *Mudarabah* contract). At present lenders, especially large institutional lenders and investment banking entities, while providing funds seek a privileged position in respect of guaranteeing returns for themselves and we are arguing that there are certainly no economic grounds for such privilege.

2 The second major type of argument in defence of moneylending at interest which in the previous chapter we detected was the **opportunity cost** argument. This as we saw comes in a number of disguises.

   a The most basic form of this argument is that in lending funds in a specific way the lender is foregoing the possibility of generating **returns on the funds in alternative uses** and this opportunity cost needs (economically) or deserves (morally) to be covered by an interest payment on the loan. If the argument is that the lender is foregoing other possible uses of the money which could generate interest as return the argument would be patently viciously circular and so illogical. One cannot justify the payment of interest just because interest is actually paid in practice. That would be akin to justifying murders just because murders regularly occur in practice! The whole point of our discussion is to conduct a critical moral appraisal of the practice of moneylending at interest; and to justify the charging of interest in terms of other opportunities for earning interest foregone would be to assume what we are trying to prove/assess. However what could be argued without circularity is that the lender in advancing funds for a particular use is foregoing among other things the possibility of using those funds in alternative productive enterprises and so those (uncertain) returns foregone represent an opportunity cost to be compensated. This is indeed the case … but it grounds an argument *not* for payment of interest but only for a participation in the (uncertain) profits or losses of the enterprise or venture to which funds are advanced. There is in any case the awkward fact that in addition to the alternative of lending money to a productive enterprise or potentially profit-making venture, the lender could decide to use the funds for consumption purposes (for a consumption binge as noted earlier) in which case there will be no financial surplus generated. Hence we cannot, strictly speaking, say that the uncertain profitability of alternative productive uses of funds lent are *the* definitive opportunity cost of lending because by definition the opportunity cost is the value of the *next best opportunity foregone* when resources are committed to a particular use[5] and this next best use could in certain cases be a consumption binge.

b Mention of the alternative of using loanable funds for consumption purposes leads to a second variant of the opportunity cost argument which has been suggested by many commentators: the argument that compensation is needed (economically) or deserved (morally) to the extent that the lender is abstaining from current immediate consumption in favour no doubt of future consumption[6]: the **abstinence** argument in effect. The abstinence argument is evidently very closely related to the **reward for waiting** or **time preference** argument which is a key element in the so-called *agio* theory in defence of moneylending at interest. However the abstinence/reward for waiting argument has harboured an ambivalence as between an economic argument to the effect that people in practice need to be rewarded for waiting since waiting is seen as somehow a burden (and so an opportunity cost) and an ethical argument to the effect that people deserve to be rewarded for their waiting, for their sacrifice of immediate consumption pleasures. Here perhaps more than anywhere else the intertwining of the purely positive economic argument with the normative moral argument in the discussion of moneylending at interest is most clearly in evidence, the word abstinence itself resonating with subliminal moral undertones. But what are we to make of these arguments? At the purely positive economic level where it is argued that as a matter of simple fact people need to be rewarded for abstinence seen as a sacrifice which without reward people will simply not make, one has to ask the question if abstinence from present consumption in favour of future consumption is always a sacrifice or burden. For example if it is mid-December and I win or am planning a holiday to a destination such as Cannes or Rimini which are seaside resorts much more attractive in summer than in winter for climatic reasons, I will definitely prefer to take the holiday in six months' time rather than straight away. I would definitively choose to wait, to defer the pleasure rather than opt for immediate gratification. While in that case it might be argued that I defer for the sake of even greater pleasure in the future there may also be simple reasons of time management as opposed to greater future pleasure why I might wish to wait, to defer consumption until I have the time properly to enjoy a good or activity; one cannot simply do everything at once and therefore we often put off enjoyment of pleasures until we have the time to devote to them. Finally it is not difficult to imagine circumstances where abstinence from immediate pleasure is itself something which a consumer prefers: one has only to consider a person seeking to lose weight or to avoid obesity in order to look better or to avoid health difficulties: such people will gladly choose to defer at least certain types of current consumption. Hence the idea that abstinence is always a burden to be recompensed, an opportunity cost, is simply refuted. It is far from being systematically the case that people will always need to be compensated for abstinence, to be rewarded for waiting.

There is then the moral variant of the argument which says that abstinence being a sacrifice it deserves or is morally appropriate that it be compensated through payment of interest. Apart from the fact that abstinence may not always be a sacrifice as we have just seen, in a variety of moral philosophies and religions abstinence is seen as morally a *good* thing and we are enjoined to practise a degree of abstinence for our own good. In puritanical versions of Christianity associated with Calvinism abstinence from immediate material pleasures of any kind is strongly recommended and the reward for abstinence comes in an after-life in paradise. In less strict versions of Christianity and in Islam a degree of abstinence and self-control are held to be good for the soul and encouraged. In eastern Buddhist wisdom the excessive pursuit of any material pleasure is regarded as ultimately frustrating and destructive of a balanced personality. Greed is bad and we should live by a Middle Way which allows for enjoyment certainly of the pleasures of life but enjoins us also to know when we should abstain and say "enough is enough". This latter is indeed the watchword of the "sufficiency economy" principles which good Thai Buddhists seek to apply in their daily economic interactions.[7] The point here is that if abstinence from immediate gratification is often in itself morally a good thing there cannot be a moral argument to the effect that it systematically deserves to be rewarded because it is seen as a burden.

Bringing these considerations regarding both the economic and the moral versions of the opportunity cost argument based on the need to compensate (economically) or reward (morally) the abstinence or waiting of a lender, we find that there can be no such systematic argument and in fact in many cases people may actually prefer to abstain and wait to consume while morally speaking abstinence has if anything been regarded as in itself morally desirable to a greater or lesser extent in a wide variety of ethical systems. In short there is no valid argument in defence of moneylending at interest based on the supposed opportunity cost of abstinence.

We may note incidentally that the whole abstinence or waiting argument makes no sense in relation to large institutional lenders. While the opportunity cost argument in terms of returns foregone from alternative productive uses of the funds as reviewed at 2(a) above is fully applicable to institutional as well as to individual personal lenders, the argument at 2(b) which we have just discussed has no relevance whatever to institutional lenders since they are not consumers and so cannot be deemed to be somehow abstaining from current in favour of future consumption.

If there is any argument for financial institutions to charge interest on abstinence grounds it relates to the fact that as financial intermediaries they may need to pay interest to savers who place their funds on deposit with them; and in that case if their activities are to be profitable the intermediaries must perforce make a return on the loans they make that is in excess of any interest payment they make to depositors. However it will hopefully be clear that this as an argument for charging interest on loans does not stand up at all. Perhaps most obviously the financial intermediary does not need to charge interest on loans to render its intermediation activities profitable: it can just as easily adopt an approach based on participation in profits and losses of borrowers which if suitably calibrated can be fully profitable. And in any case a large proportion of bank deposits (those in current accounts) do not earn any interest whatever for the depositors: the banks are providing a safe deposit for cash in effect.

En passant it may be noted here that consistently with what we have already said about the untenability of the abstinence argument and in the light of the Aristotelian ethical norm which we are seeking systematically to defend, we would argue that there should never be any payment of fixed interest to depositors: at best depositors may be offered a participation in the profits and losses of the bank, and in any case many especially retail depositors will deposit cash with zero return just for purposes of safe-keeping.

3 Often linked or even mixed up with the abstinence or waiting argument for the payment of interest on loans is the argument from **risk**. It is held that

the lender is taking certain risks in lending and that these need (economically) or deserve (ethically) to be recompensed. If we consider that there are other alternative uses of funds which present no risk or at least much less risk than the lending in question then this can also be considered as a variant of the opportunity cost argument (by lending to a risky enterprise I forego the opportunity of lending to lower risk operations), and this probably explains why it is often intertwined with the abstinence argument, both being seen in effect as opportunity costs. But although superficially appealing the argument from risk on a closer critical examination turns out to be anything but straightforward. Take the simplest version which baldly states that lenders need to be compensated for taking risks. This assumes that all lenders of funds are in all situations what economists call risk-averse; that is to say that if offered a fair gamble they will reject it. Yet we very well know that people are more than happy also to take certain sorts of gambles *which are loaded against them*, in particular those with very small but very likely loss against a small probability of large gain (e.g. lotteries). Such behaviour economists describe as risk-loving, and it is as much a part of everyday economic reality as risk-aversion (and indeed the very same people may both take out insurance against losses and gamble on lotteries or in other ways).[8] But if risk-loving behaviour is widely prevalent in the economy across all social classes and strata (as indeed it patently is insofar as people from all manner of backgrounds are prepared to gamble as well as to take out insurance), it follows that one cannot make out a general argument in defence of interest on loans in terms of compensation for risks taken since that would be to assume that *all people are risk-averse all of the time*. This just is not the case, not even approximately so. And yes indeed, one of the great shibboleths of contemporary finance theorising, that taking risks requires compensation or reward, is thereby also decidedly shattered. It simply is not always the case that taking risks requires to be specifically rewarded; for cases of risk-loving choices or actions no such inducement is required and people may actually be prepared to pay for the privilege of taking the risks (in any gambles loaded against them in effect).

A behaviourally inclined economist may of course object that things are more complex than this simple risk-averse/risk-loving dichotomy arising from the works of Friedman and Markowitz suggests. In prospect theory as developed by Kahneman and Tversky we find a rather more complex picture of how rational human beings appear to make choices in the face of risk.[9] But one thing is for sure: prospect theory does *not* lead to the conclusion that people's choices are always risk-averse. Prospect theory rather tells us that when faced with a choice between a certain definite gain and the prospect of a gamble which has an actuarially slightly higher value than the certain gain most people will choose the certain gain ("A bird in the hand is worth two in the bush"). But the very same theory equally tells us (on the basis of extensive empirical studies) that if faced with a choice between a certain definitive loss and a gamble which has an actuarial value which is less than the certainty but where winning would entirely wipe out the losses, most people will choose the gamble (I might as well be hung for a sheep as for a lamb!). So a type of risk-loving behaviour is still present even in the prospect theory of Kahneman and Tversky, and it appears most strongly in the face of the losses lenders might face when lending to risky business ventures.

What we have therefore shown in the above is that the taking of risk by lenders may not always need or deserve to be compensated because in many cases people are not risk-averse; there can be no simplistic or general argument to the effect that taking of risks must be compensated. But our argument does admit that there will be perhaps many cases where people are risk-averse and in such cases a compensation for risk-taking may be needed or morally justifiable. However in the light of the arguments under point 1 above (at the beginning of this chapter), what would be justified in such cases would not necessarily be a fixed interest return but rather a participation in the profits or losses of the risky venture being financed. In fairness if a lender is risk-averse and is to be persuaded to become involved in a risky venture it is appropriate and indeed just that they should participate in profits and losses of the venture to the full. As things stand in contemporary debt financing however the lender surrounds the loan typically with an array of legally binding contractual safeguards which have the effect of transferring virtually all of the risks onto the borrower and certainly the aim of the often mountainous paperwork associated with taking any loan through financial intermediaries is precisely to minimise and if possible eliminate entirely any assumption of risk by the lenders (this being particularly the case when collateral or other forms of guarantee are pledged). If however lenders seek thus to participate in the venture without themselves taking no or at or at least minimal risks then there can be no argument for compensating the risk by an interest payment on top of the principal sum lent. In short there might be other arguments for interest but there cannot be a risk-aversion based argument for the charging of interest since that would be tantamount to lenders wanting to have their cake and also to eat it! A risk-averse lender could however be deemed to be entitled to a participation in profits and losses.

4. Indirectly linked to the insurance against risk arguments for interest there is also the so-called ***agio*** or **time preference** theory of moneylending at interest. In this *agio* variant the focus is not so much on the risk that the borrower could default but rather on certain risks for the lender when waiting for a return. There is first of all the risk that when foregoing current consumption in favour of future consumption the lender may quite simply be dead by the time the loan is repaid. That is of course always possible ("*we know not the day nor the hour*" …) but it is hardly relevant as an

argument for some kind of significant compensation to the lender unless one is talking of a very old or sick lender; and of course the argument has no relevance whatever to institutional lenders as corporate entities. Hence the argument is more usually intended in the sense that by lending and thereby postponing current consumption the lender is taking the risk that the goods they may wish to consume may not be available in the future. There is indeed that risk … but then the goods available in the future may be of even higher quality than those available today in which case deferring consumption far from being a risky sacrifice will actually lead to even greater enjoyment in the future. If technological progress means anything it means inter alia precisely such advances in the quality of consumer goods, services and activities and indeed given human ingenuity, curiosity and the resultant constant stream of innovation to which that leads, far from expecting deterioration of the consumption experience with the passage of time we should expect its enhancement. Once again therefore the argument for payment of interest to compensate for risk turns out to be hollow and unfounded despite the shibboleths of conventional wisdom regarding interest as a return for taking risks. As we develop our critique those shibboleths are increasingly beginning to look like some kind of ideological special pleading … but of that more later.

It will be evident that the above argument any more than the preceding one can hardly be deemed to be applicable to institutional lenders and so it would appear that in light of what we have seen so far by way of risk arguments as a justification for the charging of interest, there is little or no argument for institutional lenders to charge interest in order to compensate for risk. But reflection on the case of institutional lending opens up another quite distinct line or argument for charging of interest which hardly has application to individual lenders. This we might call the **insurance** argument for institutional lenders to charge interest. In effect it can be argued that over a large portfolio of loans there will undoubtedly be some loans which for a variety of possible reasons will not or never be repaid. Hence if an institutional lender were to operate on a zero interest basis it would undoubtedly be the case that there would be significant direct losses on the overall portfolio of lending offered. If for example a portfolio of loans worth €100 million is offered at zero interest and if 1% of these are not repaid the lender will only receive back €99 million. An argument can therefore be made that the lender needs (economically) or is (morally) justified to charge interest on each of the loans in order to compensate for the inevitable fact that there will be some "non-performance". If the business of lending meant inevitable losses there would be no institutional lenders. Now while this argument certainly makes economic and moral sense it should equally be clear that it is essentially an insurance type of argument. That is to say that the institutional lender covers itself against the risk of large losses in the case of the small minority of loans which will not perform by charging a "premium" to all borrowers. The sum total of the premia from lenders who duly repay their loans covers against the losses from non-performing loans.

However while this argument certainly has substance it also leaves some perplexity. First of all there is the obvious question of how much interest is necessary or justifiable to charge in order to insure the integrity of the loan portfolio as a whole. Is any rate of interest justifiable or should interest be restricted to a level just sufficient to compensate for the non-performing loans (plus some administrative charge)? There is also the awkward fact that many institutional lenders already in any case require borrowers to take out separate loan insurance, in which case it is indefensible to argue for interest as a type of insurance against bad loans. Moreover in today's financial markets with their extensive array of derivative products it is quite common for the originating banks who make loans to get at least the more risky loans off their own books by selling them off as derivatives.[10] A variant of the risk coverage argument might be that the charging of interest acts as a kind of deterrent to borrowers meaning that they need to assess more carefully the riskiness of their own projects before taking out loans. However this argument is tantamount to penalising every borrower for the sake of the minority who will not repay their debts (and in that sense is just the insurance argument in another guise); and it is tantamount to treating every borrower as guilty until proven innocent since it should be remembered that the vast majority of loans do get repaid.

What all of this suggests is that on a closer examination there is no valid argument for charging interest as a type of insurance premium and in many cases (those where lending institutions require that loan insurance should be taken out) to do so actually involves an indefensible duplication of charges. It would be much more transparent not to say honest to require all borrowers to take out loan insurance either with the originating institution or another; or where credit default swaps or the like are held by the originating institution to require borrowers to cover the premium on such "collateral".

5 One final micro-level cost-based argument for charging of interest by institutional lenders which we encountered in the last chapter was that based on the administrative and managerial costs of financial intermediation. Certainly for lending institutions there are significant costs associated with the assessment of suitable borrowers, of the risks associated with their projects and circumstances, with the due application of government regulations regarding money laundering etc.; and even if some of these costs can be reduced in our day by various applications of artificial intelligence and algorithms they are not reduced to zero and still remain. However the linkage between covering these costs of production of financial intermediation services and the charging of interest to all borrowers is tenuous

and not at all clear. What guarantees that the interest payments collected will cover the costs since they bear no direct relationship to each other? In fact interest charged on loans depends on the macroeconomic stance of monetary policy in a country (with all interest rates moving up or down more or less directly in line with the central bank's reference refinancing rate) plus a further add-on element reflecting the lending institutions assessment of the riskiness of the specific project (and depending on their level of risk-aversion). None of this bears any relation to the actual costs of labour time and use of equipment in the administration of the financial institution. In short it is perfectly defensible for a financial intermediary firm to seek to cover its cost of administration and management but that can, and we would argue should, be done by means of an explicit loan administrative charge related directly to those administrative costs and not by the charging of interest. En passant it should be noted that many banks today actually make explicit administrative charges to the borrower at the time of according the loans, a practice which completely undermines any argument for charging interest as a kind of administration charge for financial intermediation services.

6 Coming to the purely macroeconomic arguments in defence of money-lending at interest the first type of macroeconomic argument we encountered was that which sees interest playing the role of a **price** in the market for loanable funds. Interest is somehow the "price" for borrowing, and loanable funds are allocated to their most efficient uses in financial markets through this "price" as in any competitive market. The only trouble with this argument is that interest cannot be considered to be the "price" of funds, the price of money. If in a (fair) market exchange I want to buy a grapefruit I may pay €2; if I want to buy a new car I may pay €25,000; if I want to buy a new house I may pay €300,000. But if I want to buy €1,000 in a fair market exchange I will pay … €1,000! Hence it is just plainly mistaken to define or somehow consider interest as a *price* of money in any literal sense. Interest may be a charge for abstinence or waiting or risk-taking of various sorts such as we have reviewed in the arguments earlier in this and the preceding chapter; but it is NOT a price for money as such. A somewhat different version of the idea of interest as a price of money is that which would see it as a factor price or factor reward akin to wages and salaries as a reward to labour. This approach presupposes that money can somehow be considered to be a factor of production (or slightly more precisely as a "generic" as opposed to a specific factor of production); and so as any factor money requires or deserves a reward (again the equivocation between positive and normative argument is present), and that reward is the payment of interest. Interest is presented as a factor price in effect. We have already noted that money cannot, strictly speaking, be considered to be a factor of production (who ever produced any good or

service with money alone?), hence the idea that it is a factor of production is just false, sloppy thinking at best. Money can of course be converted into forms of real capital (equipment, real estate or even know-how) which can indeed play a direct role in actually producing things at which point we may speak of a factor reward to *real capital* … But at least under capitalism the reward to real capital is the profits or losses generated by the business in question. Also it may be pointed out that while labour, land and real capital are clearly limited in overall supply, money at least as we know it today (fiat money) can be expanded more or less indefinitely. Hence scarcity arguments to defend interest as a "price" of money cannot seriously be entertained either. Banks for example may give many reasons for not providing financing for a business loan: implausible business plan, dodgy past credit rating, political risks, suspected possible criminality (money laundering); but the one argument that banks never proffer is that they just have not got the requisite funds to lend. If the bank thinks the business proposition is promising they will *create* the necessary deposits for the business. And if concerns over minimum cash reserve ratios arise they will simply use their standing facility to borrow from the lender of last resort (central bank) to maintain the requisite cash ratio. The ultimate constraint on monetary expansion is actually macroeconomic and behavioural in nature: completely unconstrained expansion of money supply leads eventually to hyperinflation and currency collapse.[11] Once we thus clarify that interest cannot in any way be thought of as somehow a "price" of money there remains the question of the efficient allocation of funds in financial markets. But financial markets do not need interest to allocate funds. If for example we opt for a system whereby interest is replaced by a participation in profits and losses of the borrower as a reward to the lender then the comparative market returns on various ventures if known with reasonable transparency can act just as well to allocate funds. After all is this not precisely how the stock market works?

7 The second type of macroeconomic argument we encountered was that which argues that interest plays a key macroeconomic role as an **instrument of monetary policy**. As noted in the previous chapter in a purely factual sense this is indeed the case. The monetary policies of the world's central banks are usually announced and implemented today in terms of manipulations of certain base "refinancing" rates of interest (the rates of interest at which the central bank is prepared to lend funds to commercial banks in general) and indeed one of the more widely cited rules for the guidance in practice of monetary policy, the Taylor rule,[12] is cast in terms of interest rate as the key policy lever for a central bank. However interest rates per se are not strictly speaking a policy target for governments or for central banks; rather manipulation of interest rates (typically via announcements of the central bank's own lending rate to the commercial

banks but also possibly via open market operations by the central bank in bond markets) is used as a tool to manipulate money supply and more broadly liquidity in an economy; and money supply is in turn being controlled with a view to controlling inflation which is widely regarded as an economic scourge and as potentially very disruptive if it gets out of hand (hyperinflation and currency collapse). Despite loose talk in the financial press which often tends to see interest rates as in themselves a target they have no significance per se for economic welfare, whereas inflation certainly has (through its impact on consumer purchasing power especially when it gets out of hand). It is therefore inflation and not interest rates that is the ultimate target of monetary policy, and in fact the European Central Bank for example has only one monetary policy target: achieving low inflation which in turn means inflation $\leq 2\%$ per annum. This simple realisation leads to a logical point of the utmost importance: if inflation targets and/or levels of money supply and general liquidity can be controlled and manipulated by other policy instruments than interest rates then the idea that interest rates are a vital tool of monetary policy falls. Now of course as any first-year student of macroeconomics knows money supply can of course be influenced and transmitted by other policy instruments. Open market operations (often these days dubbed quantitative easing/tightening) by the central bank in any security or indeed in the foreign exchange markets will have a direct impact on money supply and it is of course true that open market operations in bonds will have *inter alia* an indirect impact on interest rates (in virtue of the directly inverse relation between bond prices and interest rates). Also available to central banks is manipulation of the legally binding required cash reserves or capital adequacy requirements for banks and other financial institutions. Finally central banks as ultimate regulators of the financial system may if they so wish apply a whole array of specific regulations at their discretion in order to achieve desired targets in terms of general liquidity, money supply and inflation. It may be true that under the influence of the set of policy prescriptions summarised in the Washington Consensus (overall views of IMF, World Bank and US Treasury in the early 2000s on economic policies)[13] in which there is strongly deregulatory flavour that the policy stance of many central banks in recent decades has tended to steer clear of such detailed regulation of the financial sector, but the possibility for such use of more detailed regulation as an instrument of monetary policy remains and the decision of whether or not to use it is essentially one of political ideology rather than of pure economics.[14] In any case it is quite clear that if interest rates disappeared altogether from the economic scene a central bank would still have quite an array of policy levers available to achieve the typical goals of macroeconomic monetary policies. Interest is thus far from being indispensable as a monetary policy instrument.

Upshot of these critiques

In the preceding sections we have engaged in a searching and detailed set of critiques of the wide array of arguments which have been proffered over the past century in defence of moneylending at interest, a century in which in contrast to many earlier epochs there has broadly been a consensus in favour of charging interest on loans. We have discovered an amazing array of arguments, some purely economic or pragmatic in character arguing that for lending and financial intermediation to occur in an economy there needs to be a compensation for the lender in the form of interest; others making out in effect a moral argument to the effect that somehow the charging of interest is morally justified: the lender *deserves* to be paid interest. While the authors of this book have no difficulty with the proffering of morally based arguments to justify money lending at interest, there is something amusing not to say hypocritical to find certain neoclassical economists arguing that interest on loans exists because the lender deserves a return. These self-same neoclassical economists have been at great pains over the past 60 years to try to rid Economics of all forms of normative discourse and value judgements so as to render it a purely positive science akin to physics dealing solely in hard facts and figures.[15] However our point may be a trifle *ad hominem* as an argument and does not necessarily mean that the neoclassical arguments in question are invalid.

However if we seek to summarise the overall picture that emerges as a result of our critique it will be clear that despite a century of apparent consensus none of the arguments hold up at all well under critical examination. What we have found is that there can certainly be a case for the lender to participate in the profits and losses of a business venture in which the lent funds are invested but not to demand a fixed interest payment.

Just for the sake of precision on this suggestion let us note that a participation in potentially volatile profits and losses is very different from having a variable interest rate on a loan. What the latter denotes is that on many loans especially of longer maturity such as mortgages, a bank may charge interest rates that vary with the central bank's reference refinancing rate. This has nothing to do with the micro level profitability of the project being financed for the borrower and is purely related to the macroeconomic monetary policy stance of the central bank. For the borrower the interest even if variable remains a charge that is fixed in the sense of being unavoidable and which *must* be paid irrespective of the success or otherwise of their projects.[16] Hence if we follow through the Aristotelian ethical logic that is guiding this work variable rate loans as just described linked to a central bank reference refinancing rate are just as unacceptable as completely fixed interest rate loans.

Rather than being a ground for charging of interest the productivity argument clearly points towards profit and loss sharing between lender and borrower as also does the opportunity cost argument in its non-circular format regarding productive returns foregone. The risk argument we found to be deeply convoluted to the extent that it presumes a universal risk aversion among people when we very well know that there is also extensive risk-loving preference and behaviour in the world; and even if risk averters may need or deserve to be compensated for risks incurred, this grounds an argument once again for participation in profits and losses of the borrowers but not for insistence on a fixed interest payment on loans. So to insist is in effect for the lender to seek to generate returns from risky business ventures while taking little or ideally no risk whatever themselves and that seems to the present authors at least to be profoundly inequitable; it is (as said before) seeking to "have one's cake and eat it". There is also the insurance type of argument for charging of interest by institutional lenders to cover the risks on a portfolio of loans, but we argued that this would better and more transparently be dealt with by systems of explicit loan insurance … and of course certain institutional lenders might conceivably be risk lovers (and so in no need of insurance)! Finally we examined the argument that interest is an indispensable element as a lever of macroeconomic monetary policy but we found that interest itself cannot be considered in itself as a policy target but rather as a policy instrument/lever and that there are a number of alternative policy levers which can equally effectively be used to achieve the typical targets of monetary policy.

What is emerging from this critique and most especially from the critique of the argument for charging interest to cover risk aversion is that in effect the charging of interest involves an abusive power relationship between lenders and borrowers. What is in equity defensible and fair is that the lender should participate in the profits and losses which a borrower may generate with a productive use of the borrowed funds. *To insist on a fixed interest payment (or a variable rate payment related to macro factors but that remains unavoidable for the borrowers even in the event of major losses) is inequitable and stems ultimately from the imbalance of power which typically exists between lender and borrower with the former invariably being in the ascendant, sometimes extremely so.* This abusive power relationship is of course most evident in the practices of back street lending and payday loans as already reviewed but it is present to a lesser degree but still unmistakably in almost any lending at interest and certainly in all lending by institutions. Please just pause to consider for a moment the position in which individual or small firm borrowers find themselves when they sign up for even the simplest of loans: pages and pages of paper will need to be signed or conditions agreed to online and *the individual who wants to borrow will have no choice but to sign* because every other institutional lender who might lend to them will be requiring a similar set of conditions to be signed. To add insult to injury many of the passages of dense legalistic and financial prose in these conditions would be incomprehensible to the average individual or small firm borrower. That is an abusive power relationship; and one on which contemporary financial regulation barely impacts.[17]

Hence the central conclusion to emerge from our critique is that the practice of charging interest on loans is at root morally objectionable simply because it is inequitable; it involves an abuse of power. In this respect the argument lines up with a long line of unease about exploitative lending that goes back to the Middle Ages and was shared also by commentators, such as Francis Bacon, Adam Smith and John Maynard Keynes[18] in more modern times; and indeed it remains the reason why all but the most diehard ultraliberals even today would say that the more extortionate types of back street lending and payday loans are morally unacceptable.

If instead we argue that what is just and equitable is that the lender should participate in the profits and losses of the borrower that immediately raises three awkward questions at a theoretical level as well as an array of pragmatic questions as to how such a system could work in practice. The pragmatic questions are addressed in the later chapters of this book but the theoretical questions we address here and now.

a There is the question of the impact of macroeconomic price inflation on the real value of the principal sum lent by the lender. This is not something which the participation in the profits and losses of the borrowers' ventures can be expected to cover and so it raises a potential question for the equity of our proposed system. When inflation is significant once reimbursement of the loan occurs the real purchasing power of the sum restored to the lender may be significantly lower than that of the sum initially lent on the day that the loan was accorded. There is in effect a "depreciation" of the funds lent out and it could be suggested that it is equitable that the depreciation should be covered by the borrower so that full restitution of the goods lent out should be made. There is some merit in this as a moral argument since in general when goods are lent it is held to be equitable that *if damaged by the borrower* reparation for the damages should be borne by the borrower.[19] However macroeconomic inflation is not in fact caused by or the fault of the borrower in any way; and even if the lender had retained the funds rather than lending them they would also have faced the erosion of real value of the funds through inflation in any case. So why should it in equity fall to the borrower to compensate for this depreciation?

   Viewed in purely economic terms this argument for interest to compensate for inflation does not stand up either. That is to say that if it is asserted that in practice lenders will not lend if nominal interest rates are less than inflation rates (i.e. at negative real interest rates) that is simply not the case. In many countries and repeatedly in different periods of time lending has continued even in conditions of negative real interest rates;[20] and in theory this is not actually so surprising since if the lender refuses to lend in such conditions they will face inflation and the consequent erosion of the purchasing power value of their loanable funds in any case! Hence any possible argument, moral or purely economic, for justifying a fixed interest charge to cover expected inflation does not stand up, and it would at best only warrant a nominal interest rate equal to the expected inflation rate (in a manner akin to the indexation of wages and/or pensions to consumer price inflation in certain cases).

b A perhaps more fundamental theoretical question which arises if we were to adopt a system where the charging of interest on loans is strictly prohibited and replaced by a system where lenders share in profits and losses of borrowers' business ventures is what would happen to consumer lending, that is lending by banks or other financial institutions of any sort to consumers for purposes of financing consumption activities such as the purchase of cars, household appliances holidays or even daily consumption needs (as often the case with payday loans). It is evident that in these cases no flow of profits whatever is generated for the lender to share with the borrower and so the return to the lender on such lending would in equity be zero. The consumer would simply make restitution of the principal sum lent out. The result would therefore be quite radical: lending to consumers for purposes of pure consumption activity would almost entirely cease and loanable funds would instead be channelled into uses which generate profit flows, into real value-adding activities; or into lending to governments. Lending to consumers could persist in the case of such spending by consumers as does generate a flow of net financial returns (profits in effect) to the consumer; mortgage lending or loans for further education, for example, could survive with the lender taking a share in the generated profit flow but loans for pure consumption activity would cease. The full details of how a financial system without interest in any form could work out in practice will be examined in subsequent chapters but for now let us ask ourselves an intriguing theoretical question: would a system in which *all* loanable funds flow into profit-generating and so value-adding business ventures or into public sector borrowing and none into (essentially unproductive) consumer lending be better for society as a whole? Would it in economic terms lead to a better utilisation of a society's scarce resources? And in moral terms would it be more desirable for people to restrain their greed and impatience and to wait until they can afford certain consumer items or activities before buying them[21]? Of course putting an abrupt end to all lending to consumers other than for mortgages and student loans would in the short-term lead to a collapse of consumer spending but such an effect would be relatively short-lived and certainly once-off as consumers would have to adapt to a system whereby they save up … and then spend. Moreover as things stand at present consumer debt overhangs to an extent to hold back consumption in the years when consumers seek to pay off old debts (a situation which by definition requires that they spend less than they earn in those years whereas in the years of taking the loans they had splurged into spending in excess of their income levels). There would also be difficult questions regarding those at the bottom of the wealth pyramid who may starve if loans are not available for consumption. But as we shall argue later when looking at the practical implications of a system with no consumer borrowing such people are only rendered even more impoverished by according them loans to which there is no corresponding income stream generated in the future to pay them off; and so the appropriate response if we wish to alleviate such poverty would have to be through welfare grants or perhaps more radical policies of education and promotion of work force inclusion.

c The third theoretical question that arises is related to the second: if we were to adopt a system where the charging of interest on loans is strictly prohibited and replaced by a system where lenders share in profits and losses what would happen to lending to governments since there is no obvious profit flow generated from government activities. However at least some government spending and perhaps most such spending in well-governed states does lead to creation of a flow of real value added for the community in which the spending occurs. To the extent that this is the case it should be possible to generate a flow of additional tax revenue from the economic growth or social value added but the payment of a return on government bonds rather than being a fixed interest coupon would have to be linked to the actual attainment (or otherwise) of economic growth or of social progress. Once again the further implications of such a system for government borrowing and so for public sector deficits are theoretically intriguing as government borrowing instead of being indiscriminate as to purpose would be forced into channels which yield demonstrable gains for growth and/or social progress[22]; whereas lenders (government bond holders) would now share directly in the results of the government's activities, in the value added or not added as the case may be. This would at once be more equitable and would lead to a rather more selective approach to lending to governments which would be better for lenders and would encourage a considerably more responsible approach by the governments themselves to deficit spending. Once again we may conjecture that in economic terms a more efficient allocation of scarce loanable funds to more productive uses might occur while moral recklessness in government spending would be reined in.

The above are matters of theoretical speculation at least for the moment and can really only be adequately answered if a system of lending without interest and based strictly on the sharing in profits and losses were universally implemented in practice (although some clues as to how such a system might work can be gleaned from countries which apply Islamic financial principles).[23]

Hence our next task will be to examine in pragmatic detail how a system without interest on loans would work in practice paying particular attention to the questions of consumer lending and lending to governments, these being the two cases where the application of the alternative system of lending based on sharing in profits and losses by lenders is most obviously problematic in practice.

What we are proposing admittedly represents a fairly radical reform of certain aspects of the financial system as we know it today, even if many of the features we propose can already be found in the practices of Islamic finance. More cynically inclined critics clothing themselves in a supposed worldly realism will point to the inherent conservatism and inertial resistance to any kind of reform that hallmarks the world of finance and which is only strengthened by the lobbying and covert power of the financial sector. While such resistance to change and to regulation of any kind is real and deeply rooted in the world of finance the possibility of reform is not entirely Utopian. Recent decades especially after the Great Financial Crisis of 2008 have witnessed the timid but real emergence of various initiatives of ethical finance and some banks and financial intermediaries have revised their business strategies to reflect this. This can be seen in three ways: (a) banks may decide to devote a small proportion of their annual profits to philanthropic causes; (b) lending to firms which have a specific commitment to being socially responsible and/or contributing to social progress in a community (e.g. financing investments in green renewable energies and energy transition); (c) refusing to provide any loans or financial services to entities engaged in activities which violate certain ethical principles which the bank or intermediary chooses to uphold (e.g. refusing to finance arms manufacture). The fact that there are these detectable shoots of an emergent ethical finance does not in any way reduce the force or validity of the arguments that we are making here regarding the charging of interest on loans. Those argument stand on their own feet and are in no way diminished, for example, by banks doing philanthropy or lending to investments which meet ESG[24] criteria. Rather we would argue that the abolition of interest charges must be an integral part of any system of ethical finance. The emergence of ethical finance signals however an important opening to critical reflection on the role of the financial sector in contemporary capitalism and our suggestions can be seen as surfing on this wave.

Notes

1 Friedman, M. (1970). The social responsibility of business is to increase profits. *New York Times Magazine*, 13 September 1970.

2 Böhm-Bawerk, E. (1890) *Capital and Interest*. London. Macmillan.

3 See Marx, K. (1992). *Capital*, Volume 1. London: Penguin Classics, where Marx outlines his theory of circulation, of surplus value and of the ultimate motive of the capitalist in this circulation, the accumulation of ever more wealth.

4 It might be objected that while participation in profits/losses does not block the advancement of loanable funds to productive business uses it would to some extent discourage such flows. That could be the case but it is essentially an empirical question to discover how much disincentive to lending would be created by a system which allowed returns only in the form of profit/loss sharing. The undoubted viability of Islamic finance as well as the historically large share of equity financing in German bank lending to business suggest that the disincentive effect is limited.

5 For elaboration of the notion of opportunity cost, see any basic economics textbook; for example, Sloman, J., Garratt, D., & Guest, J. (2022). *Economics,* 11th ed. Harlow: Pearson Prentice Hall: chapter 6.

6 For Puritans of Calvinist persuasion the future reward for abstinence from current consumption comes of course in an after-life in Paradise.

7 For a simple account of Thai sufficiency economy principles and their roots in Buddhist wisdom, see O'Sullivan, P., Allington, N., & Esposito, M. (2015). *The Philosophy Politics and Economics of Finance in the 21st Century: From Hubris to Disgrace*. London: Routledge: Chapter 14.

8 The theory as outlined here will be recognised as the economic theory of choices under risk as outlined in the works of Friedman and Savage and refined by Markowitz. See for example Friedman, M., & Savage, L. (1948). The Utility Analysis of Choices Involving Risk. *Journal of Political Economy* 56:279–304; and Markowitz, H. (1952). The Utility of Wealth. *Journal of Political Economy* 60:151–158.

9 See Kahneman, D., & Tversky, A. (1979). Prospect Theory: An Analysis of Decisions under Risk. *Econometrica* 47(2):263–291.

10 Such as the now infamous "mortgage backed securities" used extensively in the US in the lead-up to the 2008 financial crisis as originating banks sold off subprime mortgages to largely unsuspecting investors. It is also the case that banks in effect "insure" themselves through credit default swaps but here there is a "premium" to be paid by the originating bank.

11 The processes of money creation with contemporary fiat currencies have often been opaque and misunderstood. The Austrian School of economists from Ludwig von Mises onwards have sought to lay bare the essential nature of these processes and to suggest alternatives such as 100% cash reserves … which would completely overturn the present processes. The Austrians also suggest that the current system of fiat money creation raises big ethical issues but these are of a different nature to the unethical nature of interest charging which is our focus in this book. On the Austrian approach, see Hülsmann, J. (2008). *The Ethics of Money Production*. Auburn, AL: Ludwig von Mises Institute.

12 The Taylor rule stipulates how a central bank should set its own nominal base rate of interest with a view to attain an inflation rate target. It was introduced by John Taylor as a reliable rule for guidance of monetary policy in politically independent central banks; Taylor, J. B. (1993). Discretion versus Policy Rules in practice. *Carnegie Rochester Conference Series on Public Policy* 39:195–214; available online at http://web.stanford.edu/~johntayl/Papers/Discretion.PDF. See also Sloman et al. (2022) *Economics*, op.cit. at pgs 821–823 for a simple basic outline of the Taylor rule. Specifically Taylor suggests that the nominal base rate of interest *it* should be set by a central bank so as to respond to divergences of actual inflation rates π_t from *target* inflation rates π_t^* and of actual Gross Domestic Product (GDP) y_t from *potential* (full employment) GDP. y_t^*; r_t^* is the estimated equilibrium real rate of interest in the overall market for loanable funds: this leads to the Taylor formula for setting the nominal base rate of interest as follows:

$$i_t = \pi_t^* + r_t^* + a_\pi(\pi_t - \pi_t^*) + a_y(y_t - \bar{y}_t)$$

13 Williamson, J. (1990). "What Washington Means by Policy Reform". In Williamson, J. (ed), *Latin American Adjustment: How Much Has Happened.* Washington, DC: Institute for International Economics, pp. 7–20.

14 It is of course interesting to note that certain countries, which for example retained a much tighter control and regulation of the mortgage lending market, such as France and Germany did not face mortgage lending crises such as those of the subprime lending in the US or its first cousins in the UK and Ireland (non-status mortgages).

15 The classic statement of this position is to be found in Friedman, M. (1953). *Essays in Positive Economics*. University of Chicago Press. See Chapter 1 "The Methodology of Positive Economics". The same position has been repeated in a whole series of subsequent mainstream textbooks of the subject; see, for example, Lipsey, R., & Chrystal, A. (2011). *Economics*, 12th ed. Oxford University Press. Chapter 1.

16 Putting the point in terms of the classification of factor rewards that is common in the management literature we are advocating in effect that returns to lenders should pass from being contracted as factors of production with a reward that is fixed in advance to being factors of production participating in such residual surpluses as are generated after factors with ex ante fixed rewards are remunerated. Lenders would in effect as already noted become passive entrepreneurs.

17 Some regulation does exist for example in respect of clarity in statements of interest rate as an annual percentage rate in many countries or in mandatory "cooling off" periods when signing up to loans. But the regulation barely scrapes the surface of the problem of comprehension. It is the view of the authors that the abusive power relationship in terms of incomprehensible loan conditions can only be ended by a strict regulation requiring all loan conditions to be capable of being written on one page of A4 paper in font size 12 and in a language capable of being immediately understood by a person of average education in the society adopting the regulation. The extensive pages and pages of conditions typically imposed are nothing other than the lender trying to minimise or to avoid all risk in lending and as already argued in the main text of this chapter that is inequitable and directly symptomatic of the abuse of power by lenders.

18 Keynes occasional musings on the topic can be found for example in Keynes, J. M. (1931). *Essays in Persuasion*. London: Macmillan. See in particular the essay on "Economic Possibilities for our grandchildren".

19 It may be recalled that in Chapter 2 we saw that this was the only legitimate source of "interest" in Roman Law. See pg 12.

20 This is now extensively documented and a well-known phenomenon to economists. See, for example, Orr, A., Edey, M., & Kennedy, M. (1995). Real Long-Term Interest Rates: The Evidence from Pooled Time Series. *OECD Economic Studies* 25:76–105, available at http://www.oecd.org/economy/monetary/15173280.pdf For a very simple exposition see also http://econbrowser.com/archives/2010/10/negative_real_i accessed 18 July 2024

21 To any German speaker the answer to that last rhetorical question is obvious and immediate: of course one waits. Debt = *Schuld* in the German language; and *Schuld* is also the word for guilt!

22 This is in effect the principle known as the "golden rule of public finance" and it will be discussed in more detail in Chapter 7.

23 We should note that while there are certain countries which adopt principles of Islamic finance these are often mixed systems with interest-based lending also occurring to non-Muslims; and there is moreover considerable disagreement among Muslim scholars as to what sorts of practice are truly *halal* (compliant to Sharia law). For example there is considerable variety in Islamic views on consumer lending and many of the practices of Islamic finance in this respect look like interest charging by another name. The same is true of the payment of "premia" to savings

deposit holders in banks. If the premia are defined in advance as a promised % they are interest by another name.

24 ESG: the requirement to assess investment projects not just in narrowly economic terms (profitability for shareholders) but also in terms of Environmental Social and Governance aspects. ESG is today fading as a buzz mainly because of the vagueness and controversy about how exactly to measure in concrete cases the E S and G.

Bibliography

Böhm-Bawerk, E. (1890). *Capital and Interest*. London: Macmillan.

Friedman, M. (1953). *Essays in Positive Economics*. Chicago: University of Chicago Press.

Friedman, M. (1970). The social responsibility of business is to increase profits. *New York Times Magazine*, 13 September 1970.

Friedman, M., & Savage, L. (1948). The Utility Analysis of Choices Involving Risk. *Journal of Political Economy* 56:279–304.

Hülsmann, J. (2008). *The Ethics of Money Production*. Auburn, AL: Ludwig von Mises Institute.

Kahneman, D., & Tversky, A. (1979). Prospect Theory: An Analysis of Decisions under Risk. *Econometrica* 47(2):263–291.

Keynes, J. M. (1931). *Essays in Persuasion*. London: Macmillan.

Lipsey, R., & Chrystal, A. (2011). *Economics*, 12th ed. Oxford: Oxford University Press.

Markowitz, H. (1952). The Utility of Wealth. *Journal of Political Economy* 60:151–158.

Marx, K. (1992). *Capital*, Volume 1. London: Penguin Classics.

O'Sullivan, P., Allington, N., & Esposito, M. (2015). *The Philosophy Politics and Economics of Finance in the 21st Century*. London: Routledge.

Orr, A., Edey, M., & Kennedy, M. (1995). Real Long-Term Interest Rates: The Evidence from Pooled Time Series. *OECD Economic Studies* 25:76–105.

Sloman, J., Garratt, D., & Guest, J. (2022). *Economics*, 11th ed. Harlow: Pearson Prentice Hall.

Taylor, J. B. (1993). Discretion versus Policy Rules in Practice. *Carnegie Rochester Conference Series on Public Policy* 39:195–214.

Williamson, J. (ed). (1990). *Latin American Adjustment: How Much Has Happened.* Washington, DC: Institute for International Economics.

5 Alternatives to interest based financing of business ventures

In earlier chapters some hints have been offered of how in practice financial intermediation could work in an economy which might consider abandoning completely the charging of interest on loans or in other words all forms of debt financing. In this and the coming two chapters, we outline in more detail how such a system might actually work and what in principle would be its economic implications both at microeconomic and macroeconomic levels. Whenever one considers significant or even radical departures in economic policy or the manner of organisation of an economy reckoning what might be their ultimate impact is challenging to the extent that we are often looking at untried systems. In such cases reliance on extrapolation from existing econometric models of the economy is not advisable precisely because the new system being envisaged will involve not just, for example, setting all interest rates to zero but allied with that a whole range of behavioural and attitudinal changes as well as perhaps a significant redistribution of power in society. With such behavioural changes a whole chain reaction of further modifications in human interactions in the economy, often quite difficult to predict given human psychological quirks and biases, can be expected to occur and these will undermine the behavioural assumptions which underpin the equations that simulate human interactions in any existing econometric model. Hence perforce we are left in the realm of philosophical or at least of politico-economic speculation when looking at these issues and that defines the methodological approach of this and the next chapters of the book. However, the authors do not in any way claim to have a crystal ball and so what is offered is precisely a speculation as to how a system without interest might in practice evolve and one could certainly imagine variations on the theme of the evolution that might unfold. To attempt an econometric extrapolation from various existing macroeconomic models would also be possible but we believe that it would create false mathematical precision in the predictions and in any case given that certain behavioural parameters would certainly need to be revisited in the basic equations of the models, there would still be an inherently speculative element involved in conjecturing what those might be. However as we shall see we are not entirely bereft of indications

DOI: 10.4324/9781003546030-5

for how a system without the payment of interest on loans might pan out in practice since such a system already to an extent exists in Islamic banking and finance.

In developing the argument we shall find that the proposal of abolishing interest payments on business borrowings is in key ways different from the case of abolition of interest on borrowings by consumers or by governments and so the three cases are treated separately in what follows. However the philosophical logic which underpins our practical suggestions and speculations remains the same in each of the three applications: we consider that in each case the charging of interest involves a morally questionable demand by lenders for a fixed interest charge irrespective of project outcome which as we already suggested in Chapter 4 reflects ultimately what can be considered to be an abusive and often brutal power relationship with the borrowers.

Business borrowing: taking a cue from Islamic finance

As we have mentioned in earlier chapters if the charging of interest on borrowings by businesses were abolished this would not mean that lending to businesses through the processes of financial intermediation would stop or even be significantly affected in volume. Provided the payment of interest is replaced by a system whereby instead of the fixed interest payment the lender receives a variable return in the form of participation in profits and losses of the business there is no economic reason why such lending should not continue. It may be that some potential lenders might be put off by the riskiness of the profit and loss sharing by comparison with having their (almost) guaranteed interest payment but we should note that even debt financing at fixed interest is not without risks to lenders (since the business as a whole may go completely bust with not even the most secured creditors receiving anything significant upon liquidation). Furthermore as we explained in an earlier chapter when discussing some of the rationales that have been offered for the charging of interest, the presumption that all lenders are inherently risk-averse is untenable. People may also be risk loving actually seeking out opportunities for gambles that offer large potential gains preferably for fairly low potential losses and, one may conjecture, there are many such people active in financial markets given the appetite for risk that is implicit in so many derivative assets and in particular in the appetite for credit default swaps (where the seller of protection against default is willingly taking over risks from the buyer of the default protection). More generally one could observe that in all human life there is risk and people have to live with that (trustworthiness of partners in interpersonal relationships business and otherwise, climate and weather-related risks, epidemic risks, etc.). It is in the nature of the case for most economic decision-making that estimation of these risks is not an exact sciences as it might be with a game of cards where the probabilities of any combination can be known a priori; in the face of the inevitable uncertainty regarding the future present in any decision people will need to (a) begin from a recognition that every decision in human life and so *a fortiori* in the economy is laced withs some degree of risk,[1] (b) think about their own subjective preferences in respect of risk and then (c) articulate a more or less informed decision. So ultimately while in our proposals lenders to businesses would be taking greater risks than under a fixed interest debt financing of business there is no such thing as a risk-free decision in economic and business matters and so the differences between our proposals and debt financing with interest are differences of degree rather than of kind and should not be exaggerated. Consequently on balance while there may be some redistribution of lending activity among potential lenders there is no reason to expect, for example, a major reduction in the supply of loanable funds to businesses. Finally in a world where no lending whatever at interest is possible then lenders could either lend on the basis of participation in profits and losses of business ventures … or just hoard their money making no return at all. Under such circumstances most potential lenders would probably opt to take their chances rather than hoarding everything. We return here to the observation that ultimately the charging of fixed interest is a reflection of the power relations between lenders and borrowers with the lenders seeking to tip the scales as much as they can in their favour.

A practical objection which might be raised at this point regards the collection of loanable funds by financial intermediaries from savers, this being fundamental to the macroeconomic function of such intermediaries: allocation of savings to investment purposes. Would savers cease to put funds with financial intermediaries and rather hoard their savings at home (or in cryptocurrencies) if fixed interest ceased to be paid on deposits? Surely not: as already mentioned in Chapter 4, the vast majority of current accounts held by individual savers in banks do not pay any interest but people place their money in such accounts for safe-keeping and to facilitate cashless transactions of all kinds. Moreover for such deposits on which today fixed interest is paid financial intermediaries would pay a return to depositors related rather to the profit and loss performance of the bank (as is already the case in a variety of mutual funds).

Given that financial intermediation would continue to occur with net savers lending their funds through various financial market channels in quantities similar to those currently but on the basis of participation in profits and losses rather than in fixed interest payments we may consider the likely impacts on business over the periods of a typical business cycle. In the inevitable periods of downswing and slump which are an integral part of any cycle many businesses will face significant losses as consumer and investment demand collapse under the macroeconomic impact of the multiplier and accelerator interaction (in a downward direction).[2] When facing such losses fixed interest payments may often be the straw that breaks the camel's back forcing firms into liquidation and bankruptcy; whereas if their creditors are sharing the hit of the losses rather than taking fixed interest it is obvious that the chances of facing bankruptcy will be significantly reduced. This is good news not only for entrepreneurs and managers but also for the workforce many of whom (or all in the case of a bankruptcy averted) will avoid the distress of unemployment at a time (downswing and slump) when by definition new jobs are more difficult to find.

Some commentators may at this point object that this will only encourage zombie firms and may even constitute a moral hazard by making it easier for firms to sustain losses. Zombie firms are chronically unprofitable enterprises that are maintained in existence only by various kinds of state subsidy or other special arrangement.[3] Economists, especially those trained in an orthodox neoclassical tradition regard such firms as involving a persisting inefficiency and a chronic waste of scarce resources. In the case of certain zombie firms that is no doubt the case but that is not what we were talking about above when looking at the effect of profit and loss sharing in the course of the business cycle. There are plenty of firms which in a medium to long-term perspective (over one or more macroeconomic business cycles) can be perfectly profitable and which therefore cannot be classified simply as zombies every time there is a downturn in the cycle. To do so would be to classify every firm other than those which are capable of remaining profitable even in the depths of the deepest recession as being zombies. In fact there is nothing inherently inefficient in an enterprise which during a macroeconomic downturn faces losses: the firm may be very well run and scrupulously efficient in its operations but when a macroeconomic downturn which by definition is not of the individual firm's making sets in it can face losses through no fault of its own in particular in the case of more severe slumps in aggregate demand.

As regards a possible moral hazard in the sense that firms may be more complacent about facing losses this is hardly plausible. After all we are speaking of a system of financing which would indeed allow firms to deal more easily with losses in a downturn or slump but it is still the case that the firm has every reason to seek to return to profitability, a profitability which will be much better for the firm and its employees and also for the lenders who will share in the now higher profitability of the firm as it recovers. At most the system of profit and loss sharing will soften the blow when the firm faces losses in a slump. What may be true is that firms will be more likely to undertake more high-risk investments with this cushion of loss sharing in place: but as long as such higher risk investments are in real new business ventures as opposed to in speculation in second-hand assets in financial markets, one may wonder if this is ultimately a good or a bad thing economically speaking. Major technological innovation is inherently risky by definition but it is also a key factor permitting economic growth[4] and more broadly improvement of the human condition (e.g. through medical and engineering advances of all kinds).

However what may be conceded is that moving to a system of profit and loss sharing would probably require a rethinking of some aspects of the governance of business enterprises. If lenders (individual or institutional) will be sharing in the profits and losses of an enterprise this will certainly lead to a much greater care on their part in the initial assessment of eligible borrowers/projects; and lenders would also probably want to keep a closer watch on the evolution and strategic decision-making of the enterprises to which they lend with a view to promoting profitability in which the lender now has a strong vested interest. In a sense the lenders would be involved now in the co-creation of value along with the managers and individual entrepreneurs in a manner reminiscent of what Ostrom described as coproduction and synergy in the context of public-private interactions in getting certain public goods produced.[5] This participation in strategic management for lenders can be achieved by having representatives of lenders sit on company Boards of Directors (especially on the supervisory board, the *Ausichtsrat*, in German style dual board systems). In short moving to a system of profit and loss sharing for lenders would probably imply significant changes in corporate governance with lenders playing a more active role on company boards of directors. The degree of influence that they may be assigned would likely be greater the bigger the sums of money being lent, the greater the likely variability of the returns and the greater the degree of business expertise that a lender may have in relation to the business in question. Of course there may be other more informal ways in which the lender may seek to "tend to their investments" in the firms but what we are noting is that one formal way of achieving this greater attention to the fate of funds lent to business on a profit and loss sharing basis would be through the channel of a revamped corporate governance.

If the above arguments to suggest that a system of financial intermediation without payments of interest is perfectly feasible has been elaborated on a theoretical level, there is also a very clear empirical evidence that such a system for lending to business on the basis of sharing in profits and losses by the lender can and does work effectively in practice. Such evidence is provided by Islamic finance and banking. The charging of interest on loans being unequivocally "*haram*", impure and immoral, Muslims should not under any circumstances charge interest on loans. This is a pillar of strict Islamic finance and banking; and while there has been a certain skepticism about the degree to which this is in reality the case with consumer loans, *Ijarah* or *sukuk* bond arrangements of various kinds (of which we will speak in coming chapters), in the case of lending to business ventures debt financing on the basis of fixed interest loans is systematically replaced in Islamic banking by various forms of participation by the lenders in profits and losses. Among these we can find arrangements such as *Mudurabah* (as already mentioned in Chapter 4) and *Mukarashah* (in Arabic). In the case of *Mudarabah* the lenders/investors are not in any way involved in the everyday management of the business and in that sense they are passive participants; but they will be rewarded on the basis of the profits or losses realised in proportions of these that are determined at the outset in the *Mudarabah* contract. In the case of *Musharakah* the lenders/investors are directly involved in the everyday management and operation of the business in what can be thought of as an active participation.[6] Not only is Islamic finance the only basis for banking and financial intermediation in strictly Muslim states such as Iran, but an extensive system of Islamic finance subsists and has prospered alongside fixed interest banking in certain Muslim countries (Malaysia, UAE) and even in some countries which are by no means Muslim but where non-Islamic banks may offer Islamic compliant financing to some of their Muslim clients.[7]

What all of this suggests is that there is no need for the financial brutality which lending at interest represents for business borrowers. We have shown that financial intermediation can easily survive the introduction of a system which would prohibit the charging of interest; that the volume of intermediation would remain almost exactly the same (when the only alternative to lending on the basis of profit and loss sharing is pure hoarding with zero return by definition); and that to a significant extent such a system would be much more advantageous for businesses and their employees over the course of business cycles. In fact the only thing that would change in a move to system without interest as far as business borrowing is concerned is the power relationship between lenders and borrowers which would be tipped somewhat more in favour of the borrowers although the exact balance may depend on the corporate governance structures adopted.

In effect the adoption of a system wherein lenders share in profits and losses of businesses would as we saw lead lenders, especially large financial intermediaries through which the loanable funds for businesses are lent, to pay a good deal more attention to the uses of the funds and the nature of the projects being undertaken; and this in turn would probably lead to changes in the relative power balances in corporate governance. In particular financial intermediaries providing funds would probably demand to have a significantly greater say in the strategic monitoring activities of Boards of Directors; in effect the relative power that is lost by lenders in moving to a profit/loss sharing system of financing they may seek to an extent to recoup by active participation in the corporate governance structures and processes of the companies to which they would lend. If the financial intermediaries' participation take the form of actually owning shares in the company, they can furthermore exercise influence through the Annual General Meetings of companies. Indeed when we speak of shareholder activism in the contemporary era the activist shareholders are typically financial intermediaries of various kinds who have provided funds to the company, in particular venture capital entities. Seen from a historical perspective this is in line with the primordial meaning of capitalism as a system in which the central power of decision making and command in companies lies in the hands of the owners of (real) capital. That presumption continues to prevail in all capitalist systems right up to the present day even if hedged around somewhat first of all by managerialism[8] and later by the recognition since the late 1980s of the necessity to consider also stakeholder interests as part of a growing awareness of ethical concerns in business conduct.[9] Perhaps ironically, a system of participation in profits and losses would thus through a rebalancing of power in corporate governance reassert that primordial power of the owners of capital even if the owners in question are today often financial intermediaries of various kinds: assorted investment banks and venture capital funds.

Notes

1 Decision-takers having recognised risks will need to make some estimate of its magnitude and following extensive work in behavioural economics and psychology it has been shown that there is plenty of scope for various types of cognitive bias in risk estimation including the presumption that some sorts of bonds are somehow entirely risk-free (e.g. US government bonds or German bonds). That however does not undermine the basic point about the presence of risks.

2 For a good account of multiplier accelerator theory see Puu, T. (2006). Short History of the Multiplier Accelerator Model. In Puu, T., & Sushko, I. (eds), *Business Cycle Dynamics*. Berlin: Springer, pp. 79–142.

3 For an account of the significance of the phenomenon today, see Albuquerque, B., & Iyer, R. (2023). *The Rise of the Walking Dead: Zombie Firms around the World*. Washington, DC: IMF.

4 In the neoclassical model of economic growth technological progress in the long run is the sole source of economic growth. On growth theory basics see any good Economics textbook, for example, Sloman, J., Garratt, D., & Guest, J. (2022). *Economics,* 11th ed. Harlow: Pearson Prentice Hall, chapter 23.

5 Ostrom, E. (1996). Crossing the Great Divide: Coproduction, Synergy and Development. *World Development* 24(6):1073–1087.

6 On all of this see any good textbook on Islamic Finance such as Habib, S. F. (2018). *Fundamentals of Islamic Finance*. London: Wiley; or see such websites as Islamic Markets https://islamicmarkets.com/education/category/musharakah-mudarabah accessed 19 December 2023.

7 For an up-to-date picture of Islamic finance practices in non-Islamic countries, see Aquib, A. M. (2023). An Assessment of Islamic Banking in Asia, Europe, USA, and Australia. *European Journal of Islamic Finance* 10(1): 1–15.

8 Berle, A., & Means, G. (1932). *The Modern Corporation and Private Property*. London: Macmillan.

9 Freeman, E. (1984). *Strategic Management: A Stakeholder Approach*. Cambridge: Cambridge University Press.

Bibliography

Albuquerque, B., & Iyer, R. (2023). *The Rise of the Walking Dead: Zombie Firms around the World*. Washington, DC: IMF.

Aquib, A. M. (2023). An Assessment of Islamic Banking in Asia, Europe, USA, and Australia. *European Journal of Islamic Finance* 10(1):1–15.

Habib, S. F. (2018). *Fundamentals of Islamic Finance*. London: Wiley.

Islamic Markets (website) https://islamicmarkets.com/education/category/musharakah-mudarabah accessed 18 July 2024.

Ostrom, E. (1996). Crossing the Great Divide: Coproduction, Synergy and Development. *World Development* 24(6):1073–1087.

Puu, T., & Sushko, I. (eds). *Business Cycle Dynamics*. Berlin: Springer.

Sloman, J., Garratt, D., & Guest, J. (2022). *Economics*, 11th ed. Harlow: Pearson Prentice Hall.

6 And what about lending to consumer borrowers?

While the feasibility of eliminating all payment of interest on lending to businesses is clear enough both in theory and as evidenced in practice by Islamic finance as seen in the previous chapter, the question of elimination of interest on loans to final consumers is much more problematic and as we shall see Islamic financial practices do not offer us much help or inspiration on this question. The difficulty is easily stated and perhaps revealing in its own way: apart from the special cases of mortgage lending (to consumers) and of student loans for educational purposes no stream of income or of profits and losses in which the lender might participate to replace the fixed interest payments of debt financing is available and so the type of solution that we have just seen for business borrowings just is not present. So if we want to abolish all interest on loans what are we to do or say about consumer borrowing?

The special cases of mortgage lending and of student loans

We may begin by clearing out of the way the two special cases of mortgage lending and of student loans. It will be obvious enough that where a person (or a business entity) borrows to buy a piece of real estate which is then rented out an income stream in the form of the rentals is generated. Hence if we abolish all payment of interest on loans out of Aristotelian principle there remains the possibility of the lender participating in the rental income flows and the capital gain or loss realised on the property just like in the case of loans to business with a participation for the lender in profits and/or losses. If on the other hand a person or business borrows to acquire a piece of real estate for their own usage (to live in or conduct a business) then while no explicit new income flow is generated there is undoubtedly an implicit benefit in the sense that by living in one's own property the necessity to pay rent to a landlord is avoided. To that extent there is an improvement in the borrower' spending pattern which can be put to the payment of a mortgage and a lender wishing to apply the Aristotelian ethical principle may reasonably participate in this income/benefit flow; while if the borrower hits hard times and has difficulty in repayment the bank will have to countenance lesser and even no repayments.

DOI: 10.4324/9781003546030-6

A lender can also include in the mortgage loan contract a participation in any capital gain or loss that may arise on the property.

It should be emphasised that if banks and other lenders are to share in possible losses there would then be no question of repossessing the real estate as collateral. Such a conclusion will no doubt seem shocking and even unthinkable to banks and other financial intermediaries who give out mortgage loans taking the real estate itself as a collateral which can be repossessed. However a more measured reflection as opposed to a knee-jerk reaction will show that as well as the downside of possible non-repayment or only partial repayment in certain cases there would not only be some defined participation in explicit or implicit income flows from the property,[1] there would also be also be the potential upside of participating in capital gain in many other cases. It might be objected that given the often long duration of mortgages, the system we are proposing (with no collateral) would therefore introduce a very significant moral hazard in the sense that people could take out mortgages and then just not pay them back. But that would certainly not be in the spirit of ethical lending that we are proposing: it remains the case that borrowers have a moral duty to repay the principal on what they borrow and it is only the fixed (or variable) interest element that is independent of income flows and capital gains that represents an extortion in the light of the Aristotelian norm. Thus a mortgage loan contract would still be entirely enforceable in law for borrowers who demonstrably have income flows which would enable them to repay the agreed loan and this would of course also be a moral responsibility for the borrowers.

In effect as with the business borrowings that we examined in the last chapter, we are proposing a system in which the currently typical mortgages with relentless predetermined interest payments covered by collateral with right to repossession (which almost entirely wipes out any risks for lenders) would be replaced by a system in which mortgage lenders would share to a far greater extent in the risks involved in the real estate projects in question (both on the upside and the downside if the mortgage contract is suitably and equitably defined). Incidentally as already explained in so-called variable interest mortgages the interest varies not as a function of the profitability or otherwise of the mortgage project but as a function of the central bank's refinancing rate (ECB) or in some cases as a function of the interbank lending rate (e.g. LIBOR in the City of London) and so it remains in effect a predetermined and in that sense a fixed commitment for the borrower.[2] An interesting corollary of this approach would be that banks and other mortgage lenders would take a great deal more care when selecting candidates for mortgages. As a result disasters such as the sub-prime mortgage lending spree in the early 2000s in the USA, UK, Spain, Portugal and Ireland and the eventual financial crisis of 2008 which it sparked would be much less likely to occur. Put brutally a bank which cannot take collateral and has to share in potential losses and gains would never accord mortgages to so-called NINJA borrowers (people with no income, no job, no assets).[3]

If we uphold the Aristotelian ethical position whereby all charging of interest on mortgages is morally unacceptable we may remark that financial firms and banks today often extract a double take of interest charges in relation to real estate investments in the case of new-build projects. The banks (often the same bank) lend large sums to construction companies who are building new real estate; and thereafter they will make mortgage loans to the eventual new buyers of the properties. In neither case are the banks nor financial firms taking any significant risks, and in the case that the real estate is pledged as collateral they are taking virtually no risks at all.[4]

The second special case to consider in relation to "retail" lending to consumers is that of student loans for purposes of education and training. Again if following the Aristotelian moral norm prohibiting the charging of interest there is the immediate question of whether or not there will be an income or profit stream in which the lender can participate with a view to making a return on funds lent. In fact education and training typically yield a significant increase in income stream for the borrower as a result of higher labour productivity and indeed in the economics of education spending on education and training is considered to be an investment in human capital. Hence in an Aristotelian-compliant financial system the creditors providing finance for student loans while not charging interest on such loans could participate in the *increases* of income stream that may be realised as a result of the education. If there is no resulting increase in income stream for the educated person only the principal of the loan would be reimbursable by the borrower: but at least up to the present day[5] education and training almost invariably lead to increased earning power even if in many cases the motivation for education is not exclusively pecuniary: education also of course can contribute to personal fulfilment and well-being. The exact cut from any increased income stream as indeed the definition of what constitutes a baseline above which the educated borrower can be deemed to have enjoyed an increase of income due to education would be a matter for negotiation between lenders and borrowers at the moment of taking the loan; the key point is that the return to the lender should not be a predetermined interest charge but rather some form of participation in the higher income stream realised as a result of the education/training. It may be noted in passing that the sum total of outstanding student loans in the USA and UK which are the countries where student loans are used extensively as a method of financing higher education studies amounts to huge sums of money. In 2024 total student debt in the USA was $1.6 trillion (€1.47trillion) or almost 8% of GDP with the average indebted student owing almost $40,000 (€37,000).[6] In the UK another country making major use of student loans (at least in England if not in Scotland and Wales) for financing of higher education the total debt at the end of 2023 was £200billion (€236billion° or less than 0.5% of GDP with the average indebted student owing £45,000 (€53,000).[7] These student loans are typically being reimbursed over a long period of years and therefore the interest element on the loans considerably increases the total indebtedness that the loans represent for the borrowers. To the extent that this indebtedness is becoming politically controversial in certain countries (especially in the USA) it may be noted that the replacement of fixed interest charges with participation for lenders in the realised increases in income stream resulting from the education or training financed, while not eliminating the burden of indebtedness would go some way towards rendering the huge debt burdens for students smaller and perhaps more readily acceptable since the more incomes increase the bigger the loan repayments would be (which probably seems fair enough). In fact in the most recent iteration of his proposals to reduce the burden of student loan debt in the USA, President Biden actually proposed precisely such an element of elimination of the interest on certain student loans (borrowers who make under $120,000 a year, or married borrowers who make under $240,000, would automatically receive cancellation for the amount their balance has grown because of interest, up to $20,000).[8] But it is interesting to note that President Biden's various attempts to alleviate the student loan debt burden have met with considerable resistance from various quarters including even a Supreme Court challenge to the policies brought by certain more conservative leaning states of the USA, a challenge that was upheld upheld in the event in June 2023. This actually demonstrates the degree of resistance from various financial and other conservative vested interests that can be expected to the sorts of suggestions and policies that we are proposing in this book, a theme to which we will recur in Chapter 9.

Consumer borrowing to finance current consumption

If mortgage lending and student loans can be readily assimilated into a system in which charging of interest on loans is strictly prohibited the case of lending to consumers for purposes of current consumption is much more problematic. Business lending for investment purposes as well as mortgage or student loan lending can be based as we saw on a participatory venture capital type of set-up in which the lender participates in the increased income stream and/or capital gains/losses realised by the borrower. But when a consumer borrows for current consumption (for buying consumer durables, holidays, weddings etc) there is no income stream of any kind, explicit or implicit that is being generated as a result of the borrowing. This means that the participatory approach simply cannot work: there is no stream of financial reward which borrowers and lenders can share. This in turn would mean that in an ethical consumer lending only the principal would ever be repaid; and in a zero interest Aristotelian world where there are other types of lending which can offer some returns through participation in potential profits and losses (lending to businesses and mortgages/student loans as described earlier) this would simply mean that there would be no lending to consumers for current consumption purposes. In effect if in the pursuit of an ethical approach to all lending we simply prohibited the charging of any interest on lending to consumers for current consumption all such lending would simply wither away or be confined to an illegal black market of back street lending with interest.

In the contemporary world where consumers have become very accustomed to supporting their current consumption with all manner of borrowing (consumer loans, credit cards whose balances are not promptly paid off, all manner of "buy now, pay later" schemes) our suggestion for the complete abolition of consumer borrowing for current consumption may seem drastic and against the tide of the times. But as with our suggestions for mortgage lending it may be worth engaging in a careful reflection of what might be the implications rather than dismissing the suggestion in knee-jerking horror.

Perhaps one of the most obvious macroeconomic implications of an outright prohibition of borrowing for current consumption by consumers is that more loanable funds would become available each year on financial markets for the financing of productive business investments (or for mortgages/student loans). Put another way, consumer borrowing for current consumption crowds out business borrowing on financial markets.[9] The extent of this crowding out effect is quite variable across countries since the extent of consumer borrowing for current consumption purposes itself is quite variable and given that it can take various forms including credit card debt it is hard to measure precisely. However, we can safely say that the figures for such debt in European countries can be anywhere in the range from 10% to 20% of total lending.[10] The new loanable funds that come onto financial markets in any year are the resultant of the savings rate of an economy, that is to say the sum total of household and business savings (retained profits). These savings constitute a finite sum each year and so questions regarding the efficiency of their allocation among various uses can be raised. We have seen how business investments (at least when they work out even reasonably well) will add to the productive capacity of the economy thereby generating income streams for the borrowers; and insofar as overall productive potential of the economy rises one could argue that this represents in the long term a better use of the scarce loanable funds. Real GDP per capita will rise; and this it should be remembered will make a contribution to raising material living standards and alleviating poverty provided the distribution of wealth is not entirely skewed in favour of the richest. By contrast lending to consumers for current consumption will make no such contribution to raising the productive potential of the economy and will merely increase the total indebtedness of consumers in the economy. Furthermore in a system where interest is charged on consumer loans for current consumption, since no kind of income stream is generated for the borrowing consumers whereas they have to repay not only the principal but also a positive interest rate on the loans made it follows that inequality of distribution is thereby increased. The linkage is a very basic one and will be elaborated in more detail in Chapter 8: consumers who borrow are not among the richest people in a country since the latter would have little or no need to borrow in order to consume whatever they want. It is those of lesser means who borrow; they do not generate any new income on the back of the borrowing and they pay back more than they borrowed thereby becoming more impoverished than they were before the borrowing.

Another sort of reason for seeing perhaps advantages in a system where borrowing by consumers to finance current consumption would not exist is that this would put a strong brake on frenetic consumerism and could contribute to a greater degree of voluntary simplicity in consumption patterns. If borrowing to finance current consumption were simply impossible people would have little choice but to consume less; and while this initially might be frustrating for many contemporary consumers caught up in the consumerist rat race, they might well with time be pleasantly surprised at the simplification of their lives and the reduction of stress that a more modest level of consumption with no debt burdens would represent. In particular the pressure to work long and often unsociable hours (perhaps holding down more than one job) with a view to being able to pay back monstrous levels of consumer borrowing would be significantly relieved and people might actually enjoy life more.[11] In effect as well as being morally preferable in the light of the Aristotelian principle an end to consumer borrowing would imply significant changes to people's lifestyle, to a lifestyle which while not ascetic would be more modest in terms of personal consumption and considerably less stressful. Overhanging debt with fixed interest commitments is a major source of stress especially in contemporary advanced societies both directly in terms of worries about ability to repay (not surprising when no new income stream is generated by the borrowing)[12] and indirectly by the pressures to work more and perhaps with multiple jobs. Such stress levels are quite simply bad for people's health and so there is also a good public health argument for ending lending to consumers.

In the last chapter we saw how lending to businesses on a non-interest basis is possible and is widely practised in Islamic finance through *Mudarabah* and *Musharakah* both involving participation in profits and losses by the lender. We thereby demonstrated for business borrowing/lending the complete feasibility in the practice of a system in which interest is prohibited. But of course, with consumer borrowing for current consumption there is no profit stream in which to participate and so neither *Mudarabah* nor *Musharakah* are feasible. It will be interesting to see therefore what Islamic finance may have to say about lending to consumers for current consumption. Without going too deeply into the often arcane details, Islamic lending to consumers can be based on what are known as *Murabaha* or *Ijarah*. In *Murabaha* an asset or good is initially bought by the bank at current prices and is immediately sold to a consumer (or a business) at a mark-up where the mark-up is called "profit" for the bank. If the bank thus agrees to a sequence of instalment payments for the consumer to pay the marked-up price we have in effect an instrument closely analogous to a consumer loan in conventional finance.

Ijarah works in a similar way in that the good is purchased by the bank and then transferred at a mark-up to the consumer; but in this case the ownership remains vested in the bank until such time as the agreed marked-up price is fully paid up. In effect the good is leased by the bank to the consumer until the full price is paid off in a manner very similar to lease-back or hire purchase contracts in conventional finance.[13]

We would not be the first to note that both *Murabaha* and *Ijarah* look suspiciously like the charging of interest by another name precisely because the mark-up on the products sold on to consumers in both cases are based on a fixed amount stipulated in advance. It is true that the mark-up is considered to be a profit and one can argue that a financial institution must make some margin on its financial intermediation activities if it is to remain in business but the fact that the mark-up is fixed in advance (and openly stated) means that in strict economic terms it is an interest charge and not a profit margin strictly speaking. There has not surprisingly been a good deal of controversy on this question not only between non-Islamic critics who argue that *Murabaha* and *Ijarah* are just charging interest by another name; there has even been considerable debate among Muslim scholars on the acceptability of these practices.

For purposes of the argument of this chapter what it means is that if in effect we consider *Murabaha* and *Ijarah* to be in effect lending (or hire lease/purchase) at interest to consumers they are just as open to critique in Aristotelian terms as lending activity to consumers in non-Islamic banking as already discussed earlier in this chapter. If we are to reject the latter for the reasons already outlined there is no possible escape route through possible Islamically inspired financial instruments from the conclusion that all lending to consumers other than for mortgages or student loans should ideally be banned.

There remains perhaps a residual worry regarding financial assistance to people who are on the borderline of absolute poverty. If there is no lending to consumers these people could not borrow in order to be able to buy what they need to survive. Since at present such people are typically well outside of the banking system and most banks would never consider lending to them, in fact at present they often have recourse to backstreet moneylending at exorbitant rates of interest typically well in excess of 200%[14] annual percentage rates. Prohibition of all charging of interest insofar as it can be enforced against such back street usury would actually be doing such people a favour preventing them from incurring ever-rising debts or falling into debt bondage. However, it has to be said that the concern that such marginalised people might not be able to borrow in order just to be able to survive presupposes a market fundamentalist type of economic set-up in which there is no welfare state or solidarity of any kind. Our point is that given the manifest exploitation involved in back street moneylending and that banks for their part are not intended to be charitable institutions if we are genuinely concerned to prevent a section of the population from falling into absolute life-threatening poverty some kind of solution based on solidarity in a welfare state setting will have to be envisaged. Such solidarity might include zero interest loans from suitable public or non-profit entities if one is concerned about the moral hazards of simple welfare grants; and in any case if one is concerned not just to eliminate the economic deprivation but also its sources, welfare policies should also include elements of (re-)training and education in order to allow people to reinsert themselves fully in the life of a community by earning a living and gaining thereby in self-esteem. Zero interest loans would be an integral part of such a welfare package designed to alleviate the worst levels of poverty. Moreover such solidarity however exercised while it has an evident humanitarian ethical basis can also be argued to be politically imperative since societies which tolerate extreme inequalities of wealth are prone to descend into both petty and organised criminality, social strife and in extreme cases social revolution. In a word extreme inequalities and marginalisation are socially unsustainable and indeed the alleviation of extreme inequalities features among the sustainable development goals of the United Nations.[15]

Notes

1 The type of mortgage being described here is in fact closely similar to the *mushrakah* type of mortgage loan offered by Islamic banks. In *musharakah* mortgage contracts there is a form of co-ownership of the property with the mortgagee gradually buying out the bank's share and with an element of return linked to the evolution of actual or potential rental incomes. It is an application of the broader partnership in profits/losses principle of Islamic banking designed to be compliant with the Islamic prohibition of the charging of interest on loans, a principle which coincides precisely with Aristotle's moral injunction. See https://www.islamic-banking.com/explore/islamic-finance/shariah-rulings/question-answers-shariah-rulings/musharakah accessed 19 July 2024.

2 LIBOR is the London interbank lending rate, the rate at which banks remain ready to lend to each other on the financial markets of the City of London. LIBOR is not regulated by the Bank of England; it is a market rate set by the banks themselves even if LIBOR typically follows tyhe Bank of England's own refinancing rate. LIBOR is the reference rate for a vast amount of variable rate mortgages. Within the last decade a major scandal emerged whereby the biggest banks acting on the London financial markets were in effect in a cartel type arrangement agreeing among themselves to fix this rate in a monopolistic manner. The exploitative power relationship in mortgage lending at interest is only further underlined by this scandal.

3 The term was widely used in discussions of the nature of the mortgage loans that were accorded on a large scale in the early 2000s especially in to borrowers of very dubious repayment capacity and who in previous decades would not have been considered as "prime" mortgage candidates. The term "non-status" mortgages was used to describe the same phenomenon in the UK and Europe. For a brief account of how the subprime mortgage phenomenon eventually triggered the major financial crisis of 2008 see Dodd, R., & Mills, P. (2008). Outbreak: The US Subprime Contagion. *IMF Finance and Development Quarterly* 45(2): 14–18.

4 The only remaining risk for the banks is in relation to the resale value of the real estate: in the event of a property price collapse encashment of the repossessed collateral may involve some losses for the bank.

5 We insert this qualification because some would speculate that as artificial intelligence becomes more pervasive in production processes of all kinds one day there may be very much less need for many types of skilled labour (e.g. air pilots or even medical surgeons); in which case education and training for many professions/skills would become redundant. But these scenarios are perhaps overblown since we will still need highly educated humans to write the relevant software for AI applications of all kinds. We would be in serious trouble if the AI began to write its own software (and might then reasonably conclude that the best thing would be to eliminate those pesky inconsistent humans!).

6 For detailed statistics on student loans in the USA see Education Data Initiative (2024), available at https://educationdata.org/student-loan-debt-statistics accessed 7 July 2024.

7 See Bolton, P. (2023). *Student Loan Statistics,* House of Commons Library, London, available at https://researchbriefings.files.parliament.uk/documents/SN01079/SN01079.pdf accessed 7 July 2024.

8 As reported in *The Guardian* 8 April 2024, "Biden announces new plan to cancel student loans" available at https://www.theguardian.com/money/2024/apr/08/biden-student-loan-forgiveness accessed 7 July 2024.

9 A similar point has often been made regarding the crowding our effect of government borrowing. This will be discussed in Chapter 7.

10 Just as an example consider the French case where in 2022 the figure was 14.5%. See Banque de France ACPR (2023). *Les chiffres 2022 du Marché Français de la Banque et de l'Assurance*, p. 24, available at https://acpr.banque-france.fr/sites/default/files/medias/documents/20231023_web_acpr_les_chiffres_du_marche_francais_de_la_banque_et_de_l_assurance_2022.pdf accessed 19 July 2024.

11 On this theme of voluntary simplicity and overworking tendencies in consumerist societies see O'Sullivan, P., & Kraisornsuthasinee, S. (2020). You Earn as You Live as You Value: The Consumption–Work Dialectic and Its Implications for Sustainability. *Sustainability Accounting Management and Practice Journal* 11(2): 429–450.

12 There are by now many studies which show clear linkages between non-mortgage consumer debt levels and mental well-being especially in older people (over 50s) whose likelihood of generating new income streams to cover debt and interest is much lower than that of younger people perhaps at the start of a career. See for example Hiilamo, A. (2020). Debt Matters? Mental Wellbeing of Older Adults with Household Debt in England. *SSM - Population Health* 12:100658, available at https://doi.org/10.1016/j.ssmph.2020.100658 accessed 19 July 2024.

13 On the detail of Murabaha and Ijarah, see the textbook already mentioned Habib, S. F. (2018). *Fundamentals of Islamic Finance*. London: Wiley; or the various sites on Islamic finance. For example the Islamic markets site https://islamicmarkets.com/education/murabahah and https://islamicmarkets.com/education/category/ijarah respectively, accessed 17 July 2024.

14 Back street moneylending is typically carried out on the basis of monthly interest. A perhaps innocuous sounding 10% per month interest when compounded over 12 months is equivalent to an annual percentage rate of 214%. I borrow €100 today @ 10% per month will mean that if I cannot pay back in 1 month and interest is compounded for 1 year I pay back €313,84 in 1 year's time.

15 There is a vast literature on social sustainability, inequality, exclusion and poverty especially in the context of the UN Sustainable Development Goals (SDGs). On the SDGs see for example the UN Global Compact website available at https://unglobalcompact.org/sdgs accessed 27 May 2024. For a succinct overall summary of the issues and linkages between inequalities, exclusion and social breakdown see Pickett, K., & Wilkinson, R. (2018). *The Inner Level*. London: Penguin. As a recent example of investigation of the links between poverty and social sustainability see

Cuesta, J., Madrigal, L., & Pecorari, N. (World Bank) (2022). Social Sustainability, Poverty, and Income: An Empirical Exploration. *IARIW General Conference Paper*, available at https://iariw.org/wp-content/uploads/2022/06/Cuesta-IARIW-2022.pdf accessed 27 May 2024.

Bibliography

Banque de France ACPR (2023). *Les chiffres 2022 du Marché Français de la Banque et de l'Assurance*, p. 24, available at https://acpr.banque-france.fr/sites/default/files/medias/documents/20231023_web_acpr_les_chiffres_du_marche_francais_de_la_banque_et_de_l_assurance_2022.pdf accessed 19 July 2024.

Bolton, P. (2023). *Student Loan Statistics,* House of Commons Library, London, available at https://researchbriefings.files.parliament.uk/documents/SN01079/SN01079.pdf accessed 7 July 2024.

Dodd, R., & Mills, P. (2008). Outbreak: The US Subprime Contagion. *IMF Finance and Development Quarterly* 45(2): 14–18.

Education Data Initiative website (2024). Available at https://educationdata.org/student-loan-debt-statistics accessed 7 July 2024.

Habib, S. F. (2018). *Fundamentals of Islamic Finance*. London: Wiley.

Hiilamo, A. (2020). Debt Matters? Mental Wellbeing of Older Adults with Household Debt in England. *SSM - Population Health* 12:100658, available at https://doi.org/10.1016/j.ssmph.2020.100658 accessed 19 July 2024.

Institute of Islamic Banking and Insurance (London) website, available at https://www.islamic-banking.com/explore/islamic-finance/shariah-rulings/question-answers-shariah-rulings/musharakah accessed 19 July 2024.

Islamic Markets website (2024). Available at https://islamicmarkets.com/education/ accessed 17 July 2024.

O'Sullivan, P., & Kraisornsuthasinee, S. (2020). You Earn as You Live as You Value: The Consumption–Work Dialectic and Its Implications for Sustainability. *Sustainability Accounting Management and Practice Journal* 11(2):429–450.

The Guardian (2024). Biden announces new plan to cancel student loans. *Guardian*, 8 April 2024, available at https://www.theguardian.com/money/2024/apr/08/biden-student-loan-forgiveness accessed 7 July 2024.

7 Alternatives to interest based government borrowing and the implications for sustainability of government debt

The final category of debt financing at which we need to look as we sketch out in theory how a system with no payment of interest on loans might operate is that of lending to governments, basically government bonds of all types. Over most of the world government bonds are financial assets or instruments which pay a fixed return, usually defined as a monetary amount or coupon rather than as a percentage rate of interest. In some cases in recent years some governments have been prepared to pay a higher coupon as a function of the duration for which a bond is held by retail lenders, a type of loyalty premium but this loyalty premium is also fixed in advance and bears no relation to how the government's use of the borrowed money fares in terms of generating an income stream from which eventually to repay the bond.[1]

While the effective interest return on a bond will vary as the second-hand (resale) value of the bond fluctuates on financial markets, the coupon remains a fixed amount that has to be paid no matter how the borrower fares in the use of the financing. To that extent the lender is requiring a fixed surplus return from the borrower irrespective of the borrower's fortunes and so the bond becomes an exploitative form of lending of the sort that was condemned as unethical by Aristotle. But if we want to pass beyond forms of government borrowing with fixed return to lenders to some kind of non-exploitative lending to governments how are we to proceed? The question is a pressing one given the large volumes of government borrowing that occur all of the time. Globally in 2022 some 38% of total debt was government debt by comparison with a further 38% that was business (non-financial corporate NFC debt) and 24% of consumer borrowing (private household debt). Moreover if we trace back as far as 1950 as will be seen from Figure 7.1, the relative size of government debt in relation to business debt has remained fairly constant while consumer debt has had a growing share of total debt over the same period. Incidentally the growing size of consumer debt evident in that graph underlines the importance of the consideration of such debt that we carried out in Chapter 6.

As we have seen with business lending in Chapter 5, the most obvious way to operate an equitable and ethical lending while following the Aristotelian

DOI: 10.4324/9781003546030-7

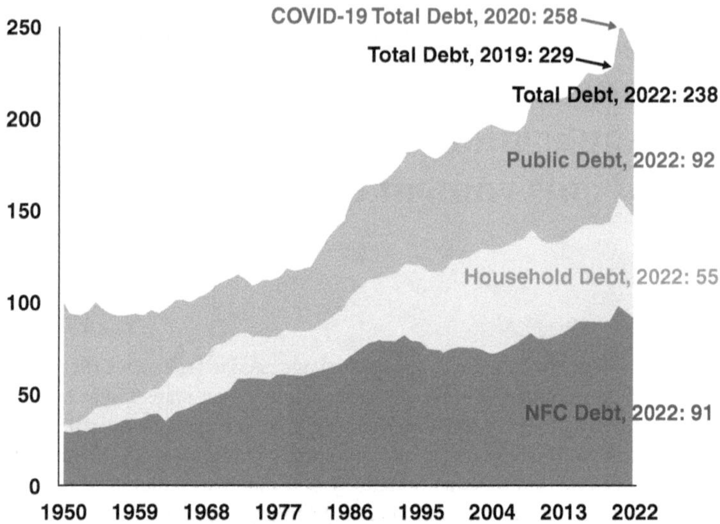

Figure 7.1 Global Public and Private Debt 1950–2022 as % of GDP

Source: International Monetary Fund (IMF) Global Debt Monitor 2023, pg 7; Fiscal Affairs dept IMF

norms would be to have some sort of participatory arrangement for the lender. But whereas business borrowers will (at least usually) be able to generate a profit stream in which participation can be offered to lenders to replace interest, there is no such obvious stream of income in which to share in the case of government borrowings. That is not to suggest that government borrowing is necessarily unproductive because certain types of government spending may contribute quite significantly to increasing the productive potential of an economy in the same way as business investments in real capital equipment or in new real estate/real estate refurbishment.

The most clear-cut example of such government spending adding to productive potential would be public investment in various kinds of infrastructures such as new fibre optic networks or new railway lines: the former in particular contribute in a very direct way to business potential. But we can also have investments which while they may not contribute to material production of goods and services in any direct way nonetheless make a contribution to general well-being in a society. The most obvious examples would be investments in the arts and culture and productivity should not be conceived purely in terms of addition to GDP per capita. None of these latter productive investments by the government translate into an income stream for the government (which might then be shared); but in the case of investments that induce an increase in overall GDP growth at least, they will indirectly generate an increase in government revenues from taxation to the extent that when an economy grows tax receipts (notably VAT and income tax) will grow in line with growth of GDP. It is also true that in a limited number of specific cases governments may be able to introduce specifically targeted charges or taxes designed to pay off specific investments which may have been made with borrowed funds, this being the case in many countries with cultural heritage public goods.[2] But specifically targeted taxes are the exception rather than the rule with most tax revenue being a general purpose contribution to the government's annual budget. This suggests that if we wanted to put in place some kind of sharing in returns for lenders, one could in principle envisage some kind of share in tax revenues for bondholders by paying a variable coupon depending on the buoyancy or otherwise of the tax revenues. Of course the buoyancy of tax revenues may not just vary with rate of growth of GDP: for example, apart from raising actual tax rates so as to raise tax yield (never a popular policy and not always effective because of disincentive side-effects) factors, such as changing demographic composition of the population, drives to reduce tax evasion, changing cultural attitudes to taxation and its evasion can all have significant impacts on the effective tax yields entering government coffers at various times. But the factor that is ever-present and systematic in its impact on tax revenues remains the size and growth rate of GDP.

A similar argument could be applied perhaps to countercyclical stabilisation policies. Where in the midst of a severe slump governments impart a deliberate fiscal stimulus which involves increasing the budget deficit and hence borrowing to cover this, to the extent that the stimulus works and does stimulate aggregate demand and so growth of output in the economy through multiplier and accelerator effects, once again higher tax revenues will be generated which could at least in principle be the basis of an income stream to be shared between lenders and borrowers.

Adoption of a system of sharing out tax revenues in the above manner would represent a fairly dramatic departure in terms of government financing and bond returns and it would be challenging to define the pragmatic detail of how such a system could work. The main reason for the difficulty is that today public sector budgets lump in not just infrastructural investments and countercyclical stimuli that arguably increase GDP and so tax revenue flows but also all manner of public spending to arrive at one sum total figure for government spending which then is compared with all projected tax revenues to arrive at the projected budget deficit (or more rarely surplus) and hence public sector borrowing requirement (or capacity to reduce total debts if a surplus). As long as such a global overview approach to public sector budgeting and borrowing requirements prevails it would be difficult to separate out those parts of government spending that represent growth-inducing improvements in the productive potential of the economy and those borrowings that represent no more than plugging of holes in the coverage by taxation or social insurance contributions of current spending on welfare (or warfare). These latter offer no (or negligible) increase in tax revenues.[3] Furthermore if the different uses of the borrowings could be separated out there would then be the even more challenging task of working out how much each of these investments had ultimately contributed to the government's tax revenues. Certainly there would be no direct measure available; rather we would be talking of the increase in tax revenues that derive say from value-added tax, corporation profits tax, income tax etc. that arise from the higher growth rate that follows overall in the economy as a result of the increased activity in various lines of new business that in turn resulted from the public sector investments (or countercyclical stimuli); in short a complex inferential chain in which many other factors might also have an influence. If we could somehow work out all of this (perhaps through an accurate econometric macro model of the economy[4]) there would finally be the question of negotiation of the cut from tax revenues that would be due to the lender but that sort of issue comes up also with business borrowing based on participation in gains and losses for the lender and would in effect be a matter of negotiation at the time of issue of the bonds (as indeed with *Mudarahbah* in Islamic finance as discussed in Chapter 5). So the biggest practical challenge for a participatory approach to government bond debt financing is actually the disentangling of that portion of tax revenue increases after some such borrowing that is actually attributable specifically to the government's uses of the funds borrowed.

Given that that is almost impossible to disentangle in practice since not in any way directly observable if we wanted to have a participatory approach to government borrowing the easiest way to achieve this in practice would be to relate bond coupons to the overall increase in tax revenues by comparison with the "base" year in which the bond was first issued. Zero increase in tax revenues in relation to base year revenues would imply zero coupon on the bonds; positive increase of tax revenues in relation to base year would attract a negotiated positive coupon while negative growth of tax revenues in relation to base year would lead either to an immediate payment (a kind of social contribution) to the government by the bondholder or to a deferred payment to be made by the bondholder as a deduction from the face value (principal) repayment at the maturity of the bond.

An indirect implication of such a participatory approach to government bond remuneration would be that if a government was borrowing (or is perceived to be borrowing) purely or largely for projects that will not yield any direct or indirect increase in productive potential through induced GDP growth the prospects for getting any return on the lending for lenders through participation would be in effect zero and in such cases lenders would simply not lend to governments in such circumstances. This is a result very similar to what we saw in Chapter 6 regarding lending to consumers for current consumption purposes: such lending would simply disappear. This result however as in the case of the said consumer loans, far from being problematic would actually be a rather good outcome. It would in effect force governments into a disciplined approach to public sector borrowing based on what has been termed the "*golden rule of public finance*"; that is to say that governments would *only* borrow for purposes of projects or purposes which can be expected to increase productive potential (GDP), and so increase tax revenues.[5] Moreover if there are projects which may yield an increase in general well-being without necessarily increasing GDP such projects could be financed in the way we described earlier by specific project-based borrowings with an assigned specific tax or charge on users to pay for the said projects: examples could be natural parks into which an entry fee is charged for those wishing to enjoy its beauty; or a theatre or stadium where the initial investment is ultimately paid back by entry fees (or by a specific local tax levy). In a system without interest the only other alternative for projects or policies that do not yield any induced increases in GDP but do contribute to general well-being would be to ensure that they can and should be fully financed on the basis of general tax revenues: they should never be financed by borrowing and in a system without interest there would be no (or almost no lenders) in any case since such lending would yield no return whatever apart from maybe a sense of patriotism. That is precisely the point of the golden rule.

It is true that this approach with a strict application of the golden rule while it is a direct consequence of eliminating the payment of interest on government bonds would also imply a much more disciplined and sophisticated approach to public finance and government borrowing which could be welcome. It would require that a strict delimitation be maintained between projects and activities which generate increases in tax revenues via GDP growth (or otherwise) and those which generate no such income stream. To give concrete effect to this there would then need to be two separate budgets for these distinct activities (rather than everything being lumped into one single budget and these would have to be constructed and voted upon in parliament separately. Then while borrowing could be considered for the first budget (generative of tax revenue growth) and lenders would be rewarded on the basis of participation in the increased tax revenues in relation to the base year, in the case of the second budget it would at all times have to be fully funded by tax revenues; and in a system with no payment of interest such as we have been proposing there would in any case be no income stream to share and so no potential lenders for this second budget. Such major areas of government activity as defence, policing, the justice system and general government administration etc. would come under this second budget.[6]

Defining two budgets, or even just two distinct sections of one overall budget, would bring, among other advantages, an increase in transparency and public accountability of governments. In particular, it would be possible to: (a) better guarantee the principle of specification and so the parliamentary approval of the budget(s) would take place with a greater degree of awareness; (b) offer more information to citizens; (c) it would also probably strengthen compliance with all other classic rules of budgetary theory:[7] unity, balanced budget, non-hypothecation of revenues and gross budget principle, annuality. Having such a dual budget approach would for sure increase the complexity of public sector budgeting and might not be to the liking of some simple-minded politicians but it could certainly be implemented. It would bring both analytical clarity in the planning of public finances and public sector borrowing and a greater transparency for all concerned (politicians, civil servants and voters).[8] In view of these advantages it is moreover a policy suggestion which could be independent of our proposals for elimination of interest: there would be merit in applying a dual budget approach for any government which is serious about applying the golden rule of public finance. But if our suggestions for elimination of fixed coupons on bonds to be replaced with a participation in increased tax revenue streams is followed then such a dual approach to public sector budgeting and borrowing would become indispensable.

As with our suggestions for consumer lending other than mortgages and student loans, that is, for current consumption (we suggested that it should just be banned outright), what we are saying here for government borrowing and bonds appears at first sight radical in relation to current practices but that is not per se a reason to dismiss the idea of tax revenue related returns on government bonds. As with our suggestions for consumer lending the question we need to ask is regarding its feasibility in practice and its further effects. That the proposal is in line with the Aristotelian moral norm regarding the charging of fixed interest is clear.

Would anyone in reality be prepared to buy such bonds whose return is dependent on the buoyancy of tax revenues one might ask? Why, of course they would, in particular if the old fixed coupon types of government bonds were not available. It is sobering to remind ourselves of two rather revealing facts regarding bond holdings: (a) in the midst of the Covid pandemic when effective rates of return fell to zero … governments were still easily able to find buyers for new bond issues[9] and (b) after Argentina defaulted on its international debts in 2001, this did not mean that the Argentinian government was completely unable to make new borrowings (albeit with a somewhat higher coupon).[10] The point that these examples illustrate is that even under the present system where government bonds have fixed coupons and are often thought of as virtually risk-free assets (and some short-term bonds are even included in broad money supply measures such as the ECB's M3) actually these conventional bonds still carry *some* risk since sovereign debt defaults can and quite often do happen. One has only to recall the Argentine default of 2001 or the partial Greek default (euphemistically called a "haircut") of 2011. Also under the present system of bond financing in certain circumstances (even if a bit unusual) governments have been able to issue new bonds at prices that reflect a zero coupon. Hence if in the system that we are proposing to replace the contemporary conventional government bond arrangements with bonds which offer no fixed return but do offer a participation in uncertain tax revenues it cannot be objected that nobody would buy such bonds. Even today people and institutions buy bonds which are risky and in certain circumstances where returns on other assets are zero or negative they will even accept an effective 0% return on bonds.

Objections to replacement of the current system of bond financing with a system in which fixed coupons are abolished but where bond holders can earn a variable return based on evolving levels of government tax revenues in relation to a base year cannot therefore suggest that such a system would never work or is totally impractical. The repugnance of contemporary finance to such radical suggestions lies elsewhere: many (but by no means all) lenders, risk-averse creditors who are making their savings available through financial intermediation, simply want to minimise (no doubt understandably) the riskiness of their lending and one good way to do that is by having a fixed coupon on bonds. But what this in effect means is that the risks of potential financial problems with the lending are being unloaded as far as possible onto the borrower who may face difficulties in paying the fixed coupon (or even the principal) when hard times hit. The core of the morally problematic nature of fixed interest charges of all kinds lies precisely here: such charges imply a highly skewed and arguably inequitable distribution of the exposure to risks that seeks to load the exposure and the hardships that may ensue as far as possible onto the borrower. We will return to this theme in the coming chapter.

What has been shown above is that the system we are proposing for government bond financing with a variable return related to tax revenues cannot be dismissed on the ground that no economic actors, individual or institutional, would ever buy such bonds. We would not wish to minimise the inertial type of resistance to the status quo which would no doubt emerge if serious efforts were made to introduce a system such as we have proposed for government bonds with returns related to government financial performance. In effect savers taking up such bonds would be making an act of faith in the competence of the governments in question to deliver buoyant tax revenues whether through economic growth or other means. The competence of many governments to do so can fairly be doubted (and not just in more remote parts of the world but also in many developed countries). Therefore in practice moving to such a new system and getting savers to take up the new types of bonds would be practically challenging for sure. That being said with the vast majority of countries actually issuing greater or lesser amounts of bonds to finance budget deficits, under our proposed system there would curiously be a virtuous side effect whereby the governments with an established record of buoyant tax revenues and so high-yielding bonds would in turn find it much easier to place their bonds with savers. There would be an in-built incentive for governments to be fiscally more responsible; and as noted above, really and consistently to observe the golden rule of public finance if they wish to be able to place their bonds on the financial markets.

Arising from the above reflection on a degree of competition among governments on world financial markets in terms of fiscal responsibility and consequent ease of selling their bonds it must however be admitted that there could be difficulties in placing such new bonds if in the first instance only a limited number of countries adopted the new system while others maintained fixed coupon bonds. This would actually be an argument for universal adoption of the new type of bonds across all or most of the world's financial markets. But while only partial adoption of the new system would be challenging for the trail-blazing governments it would not be impossible. First of all there are always risk-loving individuals or institutions who may be attracted by a variable rate bond in particular if the potential upside is big enough; after all given the existence and active trading of wide ranges of derivatives, swaps and insurance products of all kinds it follows that there must be large numbers of risk-loving actors present in financial markets (otherwise the risky products could not be so widely traded) and so there will be plenty of potential takers for the new type of bonds. Furthermore there are the moral arguments that we have proposed in earlier chapters against fixed interest lending and if accepted and taken seriously these are in fact a further reason for adopting the new type of bonds if we wish to have a more ethical financial sector. Just as some countries already go much further than others in adopting policies of environmental protection essentially on ethical and sustainability grounds so also some countries might wish to lead by example in promoting a more ethical finance. Furthermore in any case as we shall now argue there is one aspect of the variable returns approach to bond financing which could be particularly attractive to governments: if judiciously managed it would be a powerful antidote to the dangers of debt explosion especially for countries that have already high outstanding past debt.

If a system of government bond financing with variable coupons related to overall tax revenues such as we have been advocating were adopted it would render government debt significantly more sustainable in the long term. As we noted earlier government borrowing does not give rise directly to any income stream which can be used to pay off the bonds at maturity in the way that business borrowing generates a profit flow which can be so used. The only way in which a government can have any hope of paying off the loans is if tax revenues rise significantly as we saw. But let us remember that it is to *extra* new tax revenues in relation to the base year of the bond's issue that the government must look to pay off the loans; after all the tax revenues that were already in place at the time of the government initially incurring the debt (issuing new bonds) will typically be needed in the future to pay for the various public services they were financing unless there is a significant cut-back in public services.

Hence to pay off the newly incurred debt the government must look to new *extra* tax revenues not in place at the time of issue of the bonds. This is in effect the problem known to macroeconomists as *Ricardian Equivalence*: bond financing today must mean higher taxes in the future if the bonds are eventually to be paid off and so the policy choice is not really between higher taxes

v. bonds to finance public spending, it is rather a choice between tax now or tax later. The implication of these considerations is that unless the economy is growing at a significant rate and thereby significantly pushing up tax revenues governments will simply have to roll over their debt at maturity of the bonds: take out new loans to pay off the old loans. Governments around the world today routinely roll over their debts (especially the most advanced countries) but in the current system with fixed bond coupons there is the further problem that unless the tax revenue growth has been sufficient to cover at least the coupon interest element on the borrowings the governments in question will have to roll over at a higher sum than that initially borrowed. Thereby the spectre of exponentially exploding government debt arises and with it the danger of an eventual default on all or part of the debt. Government debt can no doubt be continuously rolled over provided it remains at a constant level;[11] the problems of debt explosion and related spectre of possible defaults arise only when the roll-overs are for sums larger than those initially borrowed; and *that in turn arises precisely from the coupon interest element on the bonds when increases in tax revenues are not sufficient to pay at least this interest element on the bonds*. If there is no interest coupon on the bonds roll-overs could be for a constant principal sum and the debt would be (in a financial sense at least) sustainable.

It would not be an exaggeration to say that government's approaches to debt at least since the 1950s have been built up in effect on a presumption or perhaps more of a bet on continuous growth of the economy which will in turn yield the higher tax revenues to pay off at least the coupon interest element on newly acquired debts. But relying on future growth to pay off debts as well as being presumptuous in terms of the expected economic growth rates required to be able to pay off especially the higher levels of outstanding debt also implies an approach to debt redemption that is long term and indeed intergenerational (Ricardian equivalence).

It will be interesting to give a few very basic arithmetic illustrations to demonstrate these points clearly and concretely. Let us say that the current GDP is €100 billion and that the government runs a new deficit equal to 5% of GDP so €5 billion and finances this with a new 5-year bond. Let us say that tax revenues account for 25% of GDP and so tax revenues are currently €25 billion. Then for the tax revenues to grow sufficiently fast over 5 years to be able to cover just the principal repayments on the bond they would need to have risen to €30 billion (since the existing €25 billion of tax revenues will presumably still be required to cover the various public services which it currently covers). Very roughly that would imply a rise in tax revenues of €1 billion each year or more precisely an annual growth in tax revenues of 4% per annum. In short for the growth rate of the economy to permit full repayment of the bond at maturity via higher tax revenues and without any increase in tax rates the economy would need to be growing at approximately 4% p.a. (assuming that tax revenues will rise roughly in line with GDP) While emergent economies in recent decades have often experienced average growth rates of this order or higher, this has hardly been the case of advanced economies (EU, USA, Canada, Japan etc.).

In order to pay off the bond it is therefore likely and in the case of the advanced economies (which rarely have achieved such growth in recent decades) inevitable that the government will somehow have to roll over the borrowing at maturity: that is to say issue new bonds to be able to pay off the old bonds and this in practice happens all the time. Ironically while private borrowers will often face major difficulties if they wish to roll over their loans, advanced economy governments do so all the time usually with little or no difficulty. So be it. But up to this point we have only spoken of paying off the principal on the loan; there is also the small matter of the coupon or interest element on the bonds, this being a fixed element under the present system of bond issuance. Again doing a rough and ready calculation if the annual coupon on the new bonds is €200 million per annum (effectively a 4% interest rate) then over the 5-year period the government will have to find 5 × €200 million = €1billion in extra new tax revenues to cover this. Whatever about the principal if the coupon element is to be covered by increases in tax revenues that will require if all tax rates remain the same a GDP growth rate of approximately 0.5% per annum. This will be feasible for most economies most of the time perhaps but it is interesting to note that in periods of stagnation or in slumps with negative growth of GDP, if governments do not want to raise tax rates (particularly likely if in a slump) then said governments will have to roll over at a *higher* sum: at rollover they will have to borrow more than the original principal. This is precisely how government debt explosion (exponentially increasing debt) can set in and it is likely to be stronger the slower the growth rates of the borrowing economy. What is also clear is that debt explosion at roll-over happens *only* because of the coupon or fixed interest element on the bond issue and it will arise only when tax revenues are not rising sufficiently to be able to cover the coupon element. Therefore if we adopt a system in which the fixed coupon is eliminated and replaced with a variable coupon that will be positive when tax revenues grow sufficiently fast the problem of exponentially exploding debt can be entirely avoided. For many governments in the world today that would be a rather attractive outcome (Greece, France, Italy, UK, Japan … even USA)

It should be remarked that the above illustration of the challenge of potentially exploding debt in stagnant economies has taken the example of a new borrowing of €5 billion and of how that can be repaid; and we have found that just to pay the coupon element on the borrowings on the basis of existing tax rates the economy would need to be growing at about 0.5% per annum. But if there is already outstanding debt from earlier borrowings which may have been rolled over many times (this being the case for most advanced economies and many emergent as well) then there will also be the coupon element to be covered on all of those past debts that have not yet been paid off. If for example in our hypothetical economy above the country has a 100% government debt:GDP ratio and if the average coupon to be paid on this debt is at a rate of 4% then that implies generating tax revenues of €4 billion annually just to service the existing debt. With tax revenues at 25% of GDP (€25 billion) that means that a little more than one-quarter of tax revenues are serving only to pay interest on past debts. Moreover if the economy's growth rate falls below 0.5% the debt will be exploding and with the explosion of course will come an ever greater overhang of coupons on existing debt that is being rolled over.

In short even apart from the moral arguments against fixed interest/coupon lending which might induce a country to move unilaterally to variable rate bonds with no fixed coupon elements, there are also more prosaic reasons why a country might wish to make such a move in order to rein in government debt explosion; and curiously, among the economies where such a move might be particularly attractive given their typical growth rates and size of total government debt to GDP we can find some of the world's most advanced economies with large and highly active and sophisticated financial markets (UK, USA, France, Italy, Japan, etc.).

If the above arguments outline some rather practical reasons why many governments might actually be tempted by our new approach to government bond remuneration the driving force of the argument we have made is ethical and based on Aristotelian principles. In effect we have argued for the adoption by lenders to the government of an entirely new attitude to such lending whereby they look actually to support financially governments in promising public sector projects or to emerge from serious recessions with a reward that is based on the resultant of the borrowings in terms of eventual growth in tax revenues. We could even speak of an attitude of lenders that is based on a co-creation of value rather than on a hit and run exploitation of the borrowers with little or no attention paid to the consequences of the lending.[12]

Notes

1 For example, the Italian government has made such bonds available to "retail" bond investors.

2 In addition to specifically targeted taxes, certain governments have used the net proceeds of national lotteries to finance cultural public goods and the arts.

3 A small increase in tax revenues could result from welfare spending if the recipients increase their consumption with related multiplier effects. But the size of any such effect will be negligible by comparison with the effects of public investment in infrastructures which in tun stimulates new business investments in a type of Samuelson Hicks Hansen accelerator effect.

4 In the current state of the art in Economics an "accurate econometric model" is almost an oxymoron not least when we recognise that the model would need to be of the world economy in a globalised world.

5 It is difficult to pin down the exact origins of this golden rule. In recent times however it was highlighted by Gordon Brown when he was British Chancellor of the

Exchequer from 1997 to 2007 and versions of it seem to underpin aspects of EU thinking on fiscal discipline. See for example Van den Noord, P. (2023). *A Targeted Golden Rule for Public Investments,* Economic Governance and EMU Scrutiny Unit (EU), Bruxelles available at https://www.europarl.europa.eu/RegData/etudes/STUD/2023/733740/IPOL_STU(2023)733740_EN.pdf accessed 22 July 2024.

6 The insistence on never borrowing for defence/warfare is very pertinent: paying for defence spending by government borrowing has been the root of many notorious hyperinflations when the government sells the bonds to its central bank ("printing money" in effect).

7 On principles of budgetary theory, see Jones, R., & Pendlebury, M. (2010). *Public Sector Accounting*, 6th ed. London: Financial Times Prentice Hall, p. 86.

8 On the increasing importance of transparency in public finance and accounting, see Ricci, P. (2018). "Accountability". In Farazmand, A. (ed.), *Global Encyclopaedia of Public Administration, Public Policy and Governance.* Berlin: Springer, pp. 1–6.

9 This very clearly observed fact in the Autumn of 2020 for a large Italian bond issue on the financial markets was a source of much bemusement and head scratching by economists and financial market commentators … but it most definitely happened. See for example the *Financial Times* article available at https://www.ft.com/content/56e4ddaf-dcf4-4a71–836d-b2d63eb9c2d4 accessed 22 July 2024.

10 On this see Baer, W., Margot, D., & Montes-Rojas, G. (2011). Argentina's Default and the Lack of Dire Consequences. *Economia Applicada* 15(1):131–146.

11 That was precisely the insight that underpinned the old British consols: these were government debt instruments on which the principal would never be paid off but the interest coupon would be paid in perpetuity … and these instruments were not only sold in significant quantities by the British government, they were actively traded until comparatively recently (2015) when the British government decided to "buy out" the consols with suitable once off capital repayments.

12 Such an approach would be in line with the cooperative approach to business activity that is implicit in Michael Porter's now widely acclaimed concept of creating shared value and Elinor Ostrom's co-creation of public value. See Ostrom, E. (1996). Crossing the Great Divide: Coproduction, Synergy and Development. *World Development* 24(6):1073–1087; and Ricci, P., O'Sullivan, P. & Fusco, F. (2023). *The Meaning of Shared Value.* London: Routledge. On Porter's original conception, see Porter, M., & Kramer, M. (2011). Creating Shared Value. *Harvard Business Review* 89(1):62–77.

Bibliography

Baer, W., Margot, D., & Montes-Rojas, G. (2011). Argentina's Default and the Lack of Dire Consequences. *Economia Applicada* 15(1):131–146.

Financial Times (2020). Italy sells interest-free bonds. *Financial Times*, London 2020, available at https://www.ft.com/content/56e4ddaf-dcf4-4a71-836d-b2d63eb9c2d4 accessed 22 July 2024.

International Monetary Fund (IMF) (2023). *Global Debt Monitor 2023*, Fiscal Affairs dept., IMF, Washington, DC.

Jones, R., & Pendlebury, M. (2010). *Public Sector Accounting*, 6th ed. London: Financial Times Prentice Hall.

Ostrom, E. (1996). Crossing the Great Divide: Coproduction, Synergy and Development. *World Development* 24(6):1073–1087.

Porter, M., & Kramer, M. (2011). Creating Shared Value. *Harvard Business Review* 89(1) 62–77.

Ricci, P. (2018). "Accountability". In Farazmand, A. (ed), *Global Encyclopaedia of Public Administration, Public Policy and Governance*. Berlin: Springer. pp. 1–6.

Ricci, P., O'Sullivan, P., & Fusco, F. (2023). *The Meaning of Shared Value*. London: Routledge.

Van den Noord, P., (2023). *A Targeted Golden Rule for Public Investments*, Economic Governance and EMU Scrutiny Unit (EU), Bruxelles, available at https://www.europarl.europa.eu/RegData/etudes/STUD/2023/733740/IPOL_STU(2023)733740_EN.pdf accessed 22 July 2024.

8 The impact of the charging of interest on the distribution of wealth

Perhaps one of the most interesting implications of a system of lending at fixed interest because rarely if ever considered explicitly within the many discussions in ethics, business administration and political economy of interest charging and debt finance is the manner in which it can impact on inequality of wealth distribution. This will be the central topic of the present chapter. What may come to mind immediately for many readers is the work of Thomas Piketty Capital in the Twenty-First Century[1] and there may be some affinity with that imposing work. But where Piketty's argument is essentially macroeconomic in nature and carried out on a grand historical scale, the argument we are reviewing here is more basic and microeconomic in nature. Our perspective far from contradicting Piketty's work can rather be seen as a microeconomic complement to it.

The basic microeconomic inequality that can arise in debt financing

In any act of lending at interest (as in every form of financial intermediation) we must by definition have a creditor or creditors who have some degree of accumulated wealth (savings) which they want to lend on to ultimate borrowers; and typically lenders will wish to earn some kind of positive return on their lending (although we saw in the last chapter that lenders may in certain unusual circumstances buy even zero coupon government bonds). In the case of lending at fixed interest this means that those with accumulated wealth will lend to those of lesser wealth (or even of zero or negative net worth) and at the term of the lending they will seek to recoup more than they lent (principal *plus* interest). In the event that the borrower used the funds in a manner designed to increase their productivity generating income streams in excess of the principal + interest charges at loan repayment there will (at micro level) be a somewhat more egalitarian distribution of wealth at the term of the loan because while the lender ends up with higher wealth (principal plus interest), the borrower ends up with an even bigger net improvement in wealth position, at least provided the higher wealth position valuation can be maintained through

DOI: 10.4324/9781003546030-8

time. This will be instantly recognised in terms of our earlier analyses as typical of lending to businesses for productive new investments. But what of lending to consumers other than for mortgages or for educational purposes[2]? It will be clear that in the case of loans for current consumption purposes, the borrower does not generate any kind of income stream whatever and will be required to pay back a greater amount than they initially borrowed. Inevitably this must lead (at micro level) to an increase in *inequality* as the lender ends up with higher wealth and the borrower with lesser wealth than before the loan was taken out. It is entirely besides the point that the consumer may have got significant enjoyment from the goods they bought with the loan; the fact of the matter is that whatever may be their well-being, their *wealth* will have been reduced simply because no new wealth has been created and they pay back more than they borrowed. It is hopefully obvious that it would be equally besides the point if their wealth may have risen from some other source over the period of the loan; but then again their wealth may just as well have not increased or even fallen over the loan period. Hence with lending to consumers the full force of the famous Biblical warning strikes home: "*to the one who has, more will be given, and he will have an abundance, but from the one who has not, even what he has will be taken away.*"[3] We have here revealed a further fundamental difference between lending to businesses for purposes of productive wealth creating investment and lending to consumers where no wealth or income stream to repay the loan is being generated (other than in the exceptional cases of mortgages and student loans that we saw earlier).

For completeness we should mention the case of lending to governments where the wealth of the borrower to which we are looking would be the wealth of the public sector or even in some broader sense of the community as a whole. We have already seen in the last chapter that government borrowing may generate an income stream in the form of higher tax revenues if the economy grows as a result of the public sector debt-financed spending. If this higher tax revenue arises from economic growth that is in turn attributable to better public infrastructures (fibre optic or energy networks, new roads and railways etc.) then we can say that the (government) borrower has enjoyed an increase in wealth on the back of the borrowing and therefore in some sense both borrower and lender end up with increased wealth. However if the government borrowing generates ultimately little or no new tax revenues there may be no increase in wealth for the government; and if there are not even enough new fiscal revenues to pay the coupon element on the debt the government faces rather an increase in their indebtedness at eventual rollover of the loans/bonds which of course represents a negative change in wealth for the government.

In the event that there are some wealth gains for the government through higher tax revenues one could compare the relative sizes of the wealth gains of borrower and lenders to establish if inequality of wealth has increased or decreased. However, this would be a rather stilted and likely a treacherous exercise because when economists talk of wealth distribution they almost invariably mean distribution of *private* wealth held by individual private citizens; publicly held wealth is deemed to be equally available for all. Therefore the government's wealth does not usually figure in calculations of wealth distribution since it is held for the common good of all at least in theory; and in practice it is indeed true for many infrastructures or public goods, such as public parks, policing and defence infrastructures and in public healthcare infrastructures in countries which have publicly provided healthcare for all. Furthermore when governments act on behalf of the community there could be gains of what one might wish to call community or national wealth that are still entirely material, such as the preservation of the beauty of landscapes in national parks or the upkeep of historic monuments but which would not feature in any of the usual measurements of wealth distribution.

What is emerging therefore is an interesting and nuanced picture of the impact of fixed interest lending on equality/inequality of wealth distribution. Business borrowing may lead to an increase or to a decrease in equality of wealth distribution depending on the size of the productivity gain in relation to the interest charged on the loans. In the case of consumer borrowing other than mortgages and student loans (these latter as we saw in Chapter 6 can be assimilated with business borrowing for purposes of these discussions) there is no escape from the conclusion that such lending will necessarily increase inequalities in wealth distribution. If we can presume that increasing inequality from the levels we encounter in almost all of the world's economies today is politically and even ethically undesirable then we can see that there is a further moral argument against lending at fixed interest to consumers for sure; and perhaps in certain cases against lending to businesses at a fixed interest. But bearing in mind what we have discussed in Chapter 5, we can readily get around this potential inequality increasing ethical problem as well as meeting Aristotle's fundamental norm against extorsion by banning fixed interest lending to businesses and replacing it with a system where lenders would participate in profits *and* in the losses of business borrowers. In such a system lenders and borrowers gain or lose material wealth entirely in line with each other. No such replacement is available for lending to consumers since no income stream is generated by the borrowing and so a fortiori there is no escape from the conclusion that lending to consumers automatically increases inequalities.

Certain economists and politicians might at this point wish to question making equality/inequality of distribution of wealth into a moral concern. This is understandable given that neither total equality of wealth distribution (everyone having identical material wealth) nor total inequality (where one person in the reference community owns all the material wealth available) is desirable. We can usefully think of these extremes and of what lies in between them in terms of the Gini coefficient measure. Gini coefficients can be used to measure the equality/inequality of anything which is distributed across a reference population. Although most usually associated with measures of income or material wealth distribution one could equally use Ginis to measure inequalities, for example, in access to healthcare or education of a certain level or exposure to certain types of pollution. Gini coefficients range from zero to one. Taking the case of material wealth, at one end of the spectrum (Gini coefficient = 0) we have total equality of wealth and such equality would destroy most of the economic incentive to material betterment for people and lead to secular stagnation; that can hardly be regarded as an ideal situation in human affairs.[4] At the other end of the spectrum (Gini coefficient = 1) all of the wealth in a community would be entirely in the possession of just one person and everyone else would have zero wealth and even the most ardent market fundamentalist can admit that that would be blatantly unfair and inequitable. Hence ethical, economic and political discussions of inequality must grapple with the awkward truth that neither total equality nor total inequality of wealth are desirable (ethically, economically or politically). We will inevitably be seeking to sketch out some kind of middle way between these extremes.[5] Both advocates of ever greater egalitarianism in wealth (communists?) and those who would say that inequality of wealth does not matter at all (conservatives or in extreme cases absolute monarchs deemed to be the sole owners of all of a country's land and physical capital)[6] need to recognise that neither extreme is desirable and that the ethical solution is to move towards some kind of middle ground compromise between Gini 0 and Gini 1. If the present authors are of the view that reducing inequality and moving to a greater equality in the distribution of wealth is today ethically and politically desirable it is because they view the increasing levels of inequality (especially inequalities of opportunity for young people) we are seeing in so many of our societies over the past four decades[7] as being highly corrosive of social cohesion and as generating profound disenchantment and distrust of politicians and of the fairness of our societies most especially among younger people. That view can of course be challenged by those who might wish to trace their middle way more closely to the upper end of the Gini spectrum and we can of course respect that; we are not claiming to have discovered some golden rule of optimality in Gini coefficients. But we thought it imperative that we state openly our own normative preference in the matter. Also it goes without saying that if we wish to reduce inequalities there are many ways of achieving this through education, taxation policies etc., and we are not trying to say that the only path to reducing inequalities is through the abolition of interest on loans; it can however make a significant contribution we believe to building a fairer more egalitarian society.

Discussion of increasing inequalities in recent decades of course brings to mind the work of Thomas Piketty and it will be interesting to see the extent to which there are parallels between his arguments regarding the tendency to increasing inequality in contemporary capitalism and our arguments in this chapter. The similarity between Piketty's argument and ours is that both see an inherent tendency to increasing inequality in distribution of wealth in contemporary capitalism. But the reasons for identifying this trend are very different while not being at all mutually exclusive. Piketty's argument starts from the broad sweep of economic history from the 1800s up to the present and he compares the macroeconomic rate of growth of GDP per capita, so in effect of overall labour productivity,[8] **g**, with the average rate of return on *all* assets which he labels as **r**. While the latter will partly be influenced by interest rates it is certainly not reducible to interest on loans being rather a weighted average return on all forms of investment. Piketty then suggests and seeks to demonstrate from a long range of empirical economic historical data that when $\mathbf{g} > \mathbf{r}$ there will be falling inequality (*ceteris paribus* of course); and that when $\mathbf{g} < \mathbf{r}$ there will be rising inequality of wealth. Basically this is because the growth rate of productivity **g** is the key to growth of wealth (and income) for the population as a whole and so in particular for labour while **r** will determine the rate of growth accruing to owners of capital, hence to already existing and inherited wealth.[9] Hence when $\mathbf{g} < \mathbf{r}$ inherited wealth will tend to grow faster than the wealth accumulated through the efforts of work/labour; and inherited wealth being concentrated from time immemorial in the hands of a rich elite (and inheritance itself tends to increase this concentration), when $\mathbf{g} < \mathbf{r}$ the concentration of wealth in the hands of the few will be intensified. Since Piketty argues that apart from the period of rapid economic growth throughout so much of the world between 1945 and late the 1970s, under capitalism $\mathbf{g} < \mathbf{r}$ has tended to prevail and this he shows has been particularly the case since the early 1980s, hence the increasing concentration of wealth in the hands of the few and so increasing inequalities of wealth have been observable in all of the world's economies that operate under free market capitalism. Like the present authors Piketty thinks that this poses in the long term a major threat to capitalism as we know it; and furthermore to the legitimacy of supposedly democratic régimes which are increasingly "captured" and subordinated by the lobbying activities of an increasingly wealthy powerful and often corrupt oligarchic élite. As wealth becomes more concentrated the lobbying power and activities of wealthy financial interests has increased pari passu to defend the privileges of that wealth going in many cases beyond what might be considered a fair or legitimate representation of special interests to a complete domination of policy formation over many fields which can be defined as state capture. Put another way in what has been called crony capitalism a severe imbalance in the relative power and policy influence of different lobbying interests develops and makes a direct contribution to the perception that many contemporary democracies based on universal suffrage are in practice profoundly unfair due to this state capture by overly powerful financial vested interests.[10]

Piketty's is a sweeping argument carried out on a vast macroeconomic scale that is very different from the microeconomic focus of our argument in this chapter. Piketty's conclusions coincide with those of Marx regarding the increasing concentration of wealth under capitalism and its potentially revolutionary consequences although the detail of Piketty's argument is different from Marx's. Moreover there have been challenges to Piketty's grand vision as being perhaps too sweeping in its generalisations and for the fact that the argument is essentially empirical in character. Piketty states and documents well enough the tendency over most of the history of capitalism for **g** < **r** but he never really explains *why* this should have been the case. He does not offer us insights into why the economy's growth rate should tend to be below the rate of return on capital in let us say "normal" times for capitalism.[11]

Our argument in this chapter is more modest, more microeconomic in scope and seeks to offer a theoretical insight which subsequently could be subjected to extensive empirical testing. The argument makes a key distinction between fixed interest lending to businesses on the one hand and to consumers on the other. Such lending to businesses may or may not increase inequality (this depends in a distant echo of Piketty on the size of interest charges in relation to profits generated by a business) and in any case the inegalitarian consequences could easily be eliminated by replacing fixed interest lending with a variable return related to business profits/losses.

But in the case of lending to consumers (other than mortgages or for educational purposes) we have argued that such lending will irretrievably tend to increase inequality (*ceteris paribus*). Thus we have presented a simple microeconomic theory that like Piketty predicts increasing inequality at least under a capitalism that increasingly tends to (if not become critically dependent upon) lending to consumers for current consumption. As well as offering a theoretical insight that is also an eminently testable hypothesis. It would be beyond the scope of this work to present a rigorously detailed test of this hypothesis over long historical periods analogous to Piketty's but it is something we may attempt in a further study in the near future. Meanwhile some broad indication which certainly does not falsify the hypothesis if equally not amounting to a rigorous corroboration thereof can be gleaned from the graphs presented below on trends of growing private household debt in relation to evolution of inequality as measured by Gini coefficients of wealth distribution.

Figure 8.1 reproduces the graph we already presented in Chapter 7 regarding the growth of private household debt. The growing trend of private household debt is clearcut. Much of this is mortgage debt but by no means all of it. Roughly speaking mortgage debt accounts for between 60% and 90% of the private household debt in advanced economies but a lower proportion in emerging economies; but then the total private debt levels in relation to GDP are much lower in the emerging economies. Some idea of the levels and composition of the debt can be gleaned from a snapshot of the composition of that debt in 2016 as presented in Figure 8.2; AEs denote advanced economies while EMEs are emerging market economies. Clearly the ratio of private debt to GDP can be seen to be higher in advanced economies but looking at the mortgage debt share in these higher ratios it varies widely across the

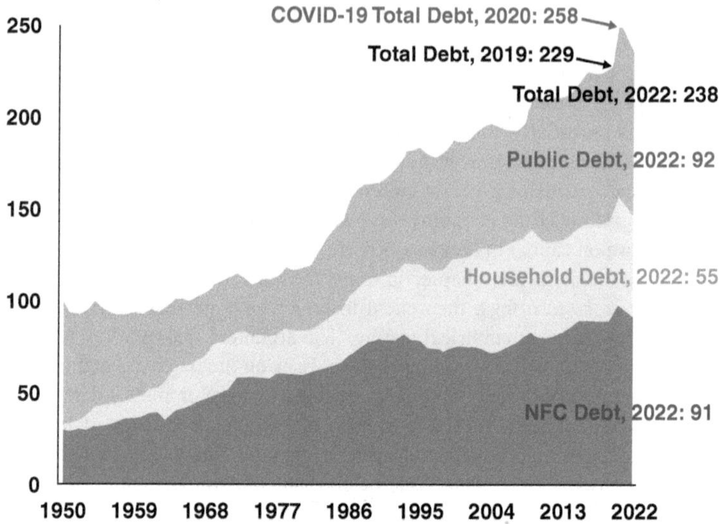

Figure 8.1 Global Public and Private Debt 1950–2022 as % of GDP

Source: International Monetary Fund (IMF) (2023). Global Debt Monitor 2023, Fiscal Affairs dept, IMF, Washington, DC. See p. 7

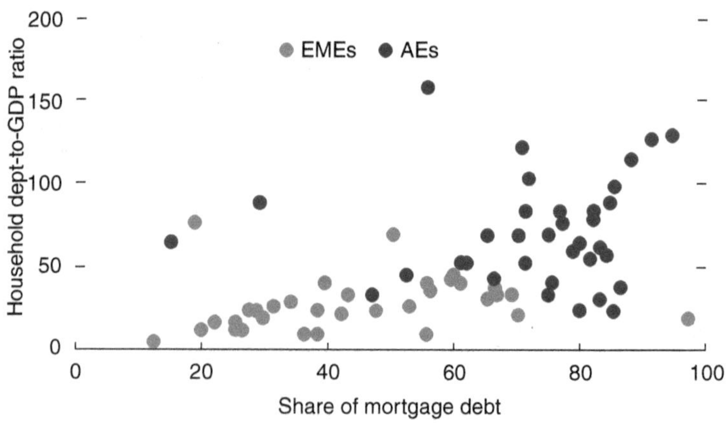

Figure 8.2 Household Debt to GDP Ratio and Mortgage Share of Debt 2016

Source: IMF (2017). Global Financial Report Chapter 2, p. 60

advanced economies as indeed in the emergent economies. There is certainly no tendency for higher private household debt to be systematically correlated with higher percentages of homeowners with mortgages. Hence when we see the significant rise in overall private household debt as in Figure 8.1 between 1951 and 2022 we can surmise that this rise is not all accounted for by greater mortgaging and home ownership; some of it will be accounted for by rises in non-mortgage private household debt; and the share of private household debt as a whole in total has been rising significantly with few interruptions since about 1985.

The final graph in Figure 8.3 presents the evolution of inequality of wealth both as between countries and within countries for the world as a whole. Here it will be seen that since the mid-1980s inequality within countries has been rising very significantly even if inequality at world level has been decreasing (but the latter is readily explicable in terms of the much higher growth rates of the emergent economies). These data are consistent with and certainly do not falsify the theory we have been proposing whereby lending to consumers for purposes of current consumption will tend to increase inequality. They are also incidentally consistent with Piketty's results which show rising inequality since the early 1980s in the advanced economies. But as noted these are

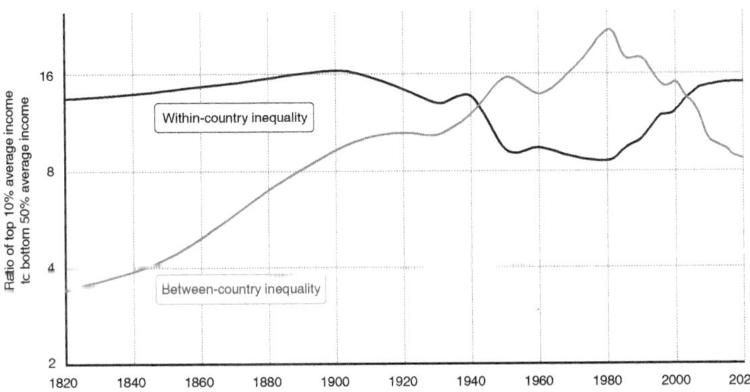

Interpretation: *Between-country inequality, as measured by the ratio T10/B50 between the average incomes of the top 10% and the bottom 50% (assuming everybody within a country has the same income), rose between 1820 and 1980 and has since strongly declined. Within-country inequality, as measured also by the ratio T10/B50 between the average incomes of the top 10% and the bottom 50% (assuming all countries have the same average income), rose slightly between 1820 and 1910, declined between 1910 and 1980, and rose since 1980. Income is measured per capita after pensions and unemployment insurance transfers and before income and wealth taxes.* ***Sources and series:*** *wir2022.wid.world/methodology and Chancel and Piketty (2021).*

Figure 8.3 Global Income Inequality: Between Country and within Country Inequality Compared 1820–2020

Source: World Inequality Report 2022 Chapter 2

only broad impressions and to establish how much of a contribution lending to consumers for current consumption is contributing to greater inequality a much more detailed and rigorous econometric analysis would be necessary.

In concluding this chapter, where we have examined the tendency for lending at fixed interest to aggravate levels of inequality in society in particular (and inevitably in the case of lending to consumers for current consumption) we should stress that we are not by any means trying to claim that this is the root of all inequality or somehow the sole explanation of the growing inequalities we can observe in contemporary societies. There are many other factors that can generate increasing inequality and concentration of wealth: in addition to Piketty's explanation in terms of growth of productivity **g** in relation to average returns on assets **r** when **g** < **r** there are more purely political and sociological factors which can underpin growing inequality. Left-wing political parties if they have sustained periods in power may be able to instigate strongly redistributive taxation and spending policies. Where there are deeply felt racial prejudices against certain subgroups in a society they can contribute to severely restricting equality of opportunity for younger people from the subgroup background thereby perpetuating and aggravating inequalities. Fee-paying higher educational systems may entrench inequality by tending to favour the offspring of wealthy parents while young people of poorer background may be very reluctant to take out student loans.

These possible sources of growing inequality and concentration of wealth may of course be of varying significance in generating inequality but they all *could* certainly contribute and for that reason we are certainly not proposing the fixed interest factor as a unique explanatory factor of the growing inequality in our societies that has been so clearly documented in Piketty's work. These same considerations also point to the need for a detailed multivariate econometric analysis of the sources of inequality taking into account all of these potential contributors over a range of countries and over a long run of data such as 1950–2020 with a view to establishing what in practice is the relative contribution of each of the possible sources as conjectured in the theory.[12] This as noted would be a major undertaking in itself and well beyond the scope of this work.

Notes

1 Piketty, T. (2014). *Capital in the Twenty-First Century*. Boston and London: Belknap Harvard University Press.

2 Outlays for education and training can be considered to be investment in human capital rather than as current consumption since they will potentially increase earning power of the educated person and indeed this usually is the case.

3 Matthew 25:29 is available at Bible Gateway website https://www.biblegateway.com/passage/?search=Matthew++25+%3A29&version=NIV accessed 12 July 2024.

4 This in fact is what "pure communism" would mean. That phrase is often bandied about by market fundamentalist thinkers such as Milton Friedman as a term of opprobrium without realising that it is only with a Gini coefficient of zero that we would strictly speaking have "pure" communism.

5 The Middle Way is of course a central conception of Eastern thinking and the centrepiece of the noble eightfold path of Buddhist wisdom. Less prominent in European thought it is nonetheless present in ideas of a "golden mean" as the guide to ethical actions. On Buddhist Middle Path see O'Sullivan, Allington, N., & Esposito, M. (2015). *The Philosophy Politics and Economics of Finance in the 21st Century: From Hubris to Disgrace*. London: Routledge. See Chapter 14.

6 Various absolute monarchs have laid a claim (usually supposedly divinely ordained) to ownership of all of the country's land and other people can at best have leaseholds. Louis XIV of France was famous for the assertion "*l'état, c'est moi*". In China there are no freeholds in ownership of land and natural resources, ownership of these is vested in the Chinese state and they can be "owned" only on a leasehold basis.

7 Increasing inequalities in all advanced and emergent economies since 1980 (especially in societies which have adopted the market fundamentalist creed) is well known and has been documented in a wide variety of studies of which the most comprehensive is Piketty, T. (2014). *Capitalism in the 21st Century*. Boston: Harvard University Press.

8 This is of course an approximative relationship and is accurate enough provided the labour force participation rate is fairly constant over time.

9 Or as Keynes would have said the "rentiers".

10 On these ideas see Wolf, M. (2023). *The Crisis of Democratic Capitalism*. London: Allen Lane Penguin Press: see especially Chapter 5. See also Monbiot, G., & Hutchison, P. (2024). *The Invisible Doctrine: The Secret History of Neo-liberalism*. London: Allen Lane Penguin Press. See especially Chapter 9.

11 Romer in particular has criticised Piketty for this absence of theoretical insight even while endorsing the overall achievements of the work. See Romer, P. (2015). Mathiness in the Theory of Economic Growth. *American Economic Review Papers and Proceedings* 105(5): 89–93. See especially Romer's remarks on Piketty's work in this piece.

12 Students of epistemology and methodology of science will detect the Popperian inspiration of these remarks. See Popper, K. (2002). *Conjectures and Refutations*. London: Routledge. See Chapter 1 in particular.

Bibliography

Bible Gateway website, available https://www.biblegateway.com accessed 12 July 2024

International Monetary Fund (IMF) (2017). *Global Financial Stability Report*. Washington, DC: IMF.

International Monetary Fund (IMF) (2023). *Global Debt Monitor 2023*, Fiscal Affairs dept, IMF, Washington, DC.

Monbiot, G., & Hutchison, P. (2024). *The Invisible Doctrine: The Secret History of Neo-liberalism*. London: Allen Lane Penguin Press.

O'Sullivan, P., Allington, N., & Esposito, M. (2015). *The Philosophy Politics and Economics of Finance in the 21st Century: From Hubris to Disgrace*. London: Routledge.

Piketty, T. (2014). *Capital in the Twenty-First Century*. Boston and London: Belknap Harvard University Press.

Popper, K. (2002). *Conjectures and Refutations*. London: Routledge.

Romer, P. (2015). Mathiness in the Theory of Economic Growth. *American Economic Review Papers and Proceedings* 105(5):89–93.

Wolf, M. (2023). *The Crisis of Democratic Capitalism*. London: Allen Lane Penguin Press.

World Inequality Report 2022, Chapter 2, available at https://wir2022.wid.world/chapter-2/ accessed 23 July 2024.

9 A call to action in face of the massive inertia of financial sector vested interests

In this concluding chapter we will seek to delineate the essentials of a plan of policy actions to transform the financial sector in the light of the main conclusions of the critique we have developed of the charging of interest on loans in the contemporary financial system. Any such call to action will of course generate a resistance from those who gain from the current system or who just may be too lazy to think about alternatives. We are under no illusion regarding both the conservatism and resultant inertia of the major players of the contemporary financial sector; nor are we under any illusions regarding their formidable political lobbying power. But as we hope our analysis has shown the alternatives that we are promoting are not actually all that radical and they already exist in a fairly robust workable form in certain practices of Islamic finance or to a lesser extent in equity-based financing of businesses by banks throughout the world as well as in the participatory structures of certain mutual societies of savers. Hence we believe that the call to action is not another vain Utopian voice destined to be swallowed up in cynical indifference by supposedly realistic financiers and policy-makers but rather is an ethical imperative with a real chance of being practically implemented, most probably in a gradualist step-by-step manner.

Building on the critical work of earlier chapters, we will now bring together all of the specific policy proposals that have been made in a single coherent list which can constitute an overall plan of action and which would constitute the outline of new and more ethical financial system. We will endeavour to show that while taken together these would imply a fairly radical overhaul of the financial system as we know it over most of the world (less so for states practising Islamic finance) it is perfectly feasible: it demands simply (or perhaps not so simply in the egotistic age in which we live) a moral courage on the part of financial actors to think beyond their narrowest short term self-interest and political courage from governments and regulators to stand up against the special pleading of lobbying vested interests. The question we must ask in the final analysis is whether or not societies as a whole would be better off in a system where the charging of interest on loans was universally prohibited and in practice eliminated.

DOI: 10.4324/9781003546030-9

Policy action 1: a comprehensive Aristotelian ban on interest

The first and most basic policy action that would be required would be to pass a **comprehensive law admitting of no exceptions whatever outlawing the charging of interest on loans or bonds of any kind**. By interest here we mean the charging of a fixed sum or ex ante fixed percentage rate over and above the principal of any loan, bond or other lending instrument; or any ex ante predefined variable rate (as in variable interest rate loans) payable by the borrower under any circumstances on or before repayment of the principal on the loan. Considering the reality of financial intermediation whereby banks of all kinds collect funds from ultimate savers and lend them on to ultimate borrowers in our Aristotelian system depositors would not be paid any form of fixed interest on their deposits but they would either earn no interest on their deposits (as is the case with most retail banking current accounts today); or they can be offered a participation in the profits and losses of the bank. If we are following the Aristotelian principle that any charge of fixed interest is an extortion because more is demanded in return than was given it might be objected that where there is significant price inflation the lender may get back less in real terms than what they lent out, then so be it: it is not the borrower who has generated the inflation and why should the financial system be set up in a manner which eliminates almost all risks for lenders? After all in periods of price deflation (which do occur from time to time) the lenders will end up getting back more in real terms and it will be borrowers who will be bearing an increased burden. Hence rather than getting involved in any exceptions to the simple rule of repayment only of the principal sum, exceptions which would almost certainly lead to abuses and subterfuges in effect to pay interest by another name, better to make no allowances for inflation accepting that that is a potential risk of loss for lenders when there is significant inflation and for borrowers in periods of price deflation.

It behoves us to remember that in human life on a finite planet there is no such thing as zero risk and we are at best talking about what is a fair distribution of risks in human economic interactions. At various points throughout the book we have suggested that the charging of interest on loans represents an unfair distribution of those risks skewed heavily in favour of lenders and reflecting arguably an abusive power relationship between lenders and borrowers.

There are however two lines of objection to the practicability of such a universal prohibition of interest which might be made. The first is that lenders will not lend under these circumstances and so the supply of loans would dry up and financial intermediation would fail. If we recall the arguments of earlier chapters, however, lending in a manner whereby lenders participate in the eventual gains or losses that borrowers experience when using the funds, there would still be ample attractive opportunities for lending. Such participation by lenders in the risks of borrowers' activities would among other things induce lenders of all types to pay much greater attention to the likely risks that may arise in borrowers' use of the funds, thereby avoiding some of the short-sighted reckless lending which can occur under the current system and which was epitomised by the sub-prime mortgage lending spree that preceded the great financial crash of 2008. In short the productivity of the usages of loanable funds and so the efficiency of the financial intermediation process would be improved.

What is true however is that with a participatory as opposed to an ex ante fixed reward system lending to consumers other than for mortgages or for educational purposes (student loans) would come to an end because there would be no potential profit streams in which to share and in a world where lending to businesses on a profit and loss sharing basis is available this would in effect mean that few if any lenders would want to lend to consumers for current consumption purposes. But that as we argued in Chapter 6 may actually be a good thing both in terms of leaving more loanable funds available for productive real wealth enhancing business uses and in terms of the reduction of individual stress for consumers. There is also the awkward fact for defenders of fixed interest charging that in periods when little other attractive investment opportunities have been available, lenders have bought up bonds with an effective interest rate of zero as happened during the height of the Covid pandemic (2020).[1]

A second and more serious objection to the proposal of universal elimination of the charging of interest is precisely regarding one possible aspect of its universality. In the contemporary geopolitical order nation states are recognised as having absolute sovereignty in the making of laws and so *inter alia* in economic policy-making and regulation. Therefore while a worldwide universal ban on charging of interest would be ideal we have to recognise that it is extremely unlikely that all countries would spontaneously agree to pass such a law or regulation however strong the moral argument deriving from Aristotle might be. Far more likely is that the new laws and regulations banning interest on loans would be adopted in some countries and not in others. Hence in a world of globalised liberalised financial markets where loanable funds can flow easily and in great volumes into and out of most country's financial markets, it might be argued that this would put the countries adopting the new regulations at a disadvantage in terms of inflows of loanable funds to their financial markets which might in turn stunt their development possibilities. That is theoretically possible but one has to wonder how significant such an effect would be in practice. Apart from casual evidence suggesting that certain flourishing international financial centres, such as Kuala Lumpur, Riyadh, Bahrain, Dubai and Qatar are also major Islamic finance hubs,[2] if we look at the share of GDP represented by FDI in the GDP of Organisation of Islamic Cooperation (OIC) countries we can see that it is in line with general world levels of such ratios. It is somewhat below advanced economy FDI inflows

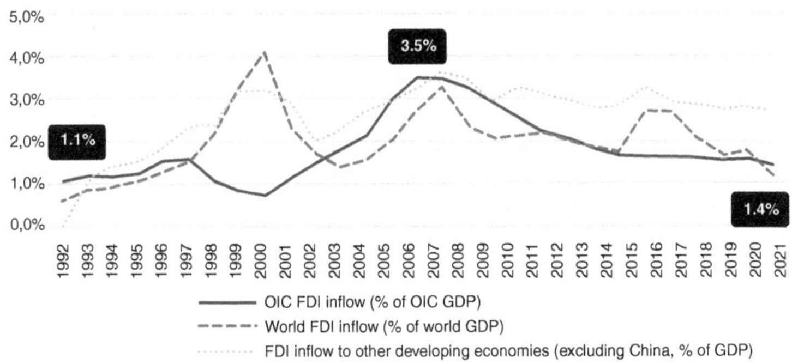

Figure 9.1 FDI inflows as a percentage of GDP

Source: UNCTAD FDI/MNE database

but that is also true of the world average FDI:GDP flow ratios; and since most of the OIC states are certainly not advanced economies the relevant comparison for our purposes is with the world average (the dashed dotted line in the diagram of Figure 9.1) Therefore prima facie there is no evidence that Islamic finance with its moderately strict prohibition of charging of interest on loans is creating obstacles to inward investment flows to financial markets where there are Islamic finance based restrictions in charging of interest in a world of open capital markets where the majority of financial markets are not Islamic (see Figure 9.1).[3]

It might be countered with some validity that the principles of Islamic finance when applied in practice may not be as strict as the outright prohibition that we are proposing, in particular in transactions involving non-Muslims or more generally in the instruments of *Murabaha* and *Ijarah* which are used for lending to consumers for current consumption in Islamic financial systems.[4] But it is nonetheless striking that there is no discernible difference in average FDI flows over time into financial markets in OIC countries which apply more or less strict principles of Islamic finance by comparison with world average FDI flows in relation to GDP.

Furthermore in Chapter 7 when discussing forms of government bond lending based on participation in tax revenues rather than on fixed coupons, we discussed briefly the question of a non-universal move away from the fixed coupon system with just a limited number of states applying the new variable return participatory type of bonds. We noted that while this would discourage the more risk-averse potential buyers of such bonds it would be unlikely to discourage completely all lending to governments offering such bonds partly because a return would still be available on the bonds (it would just not be a fixed "guaranteed" return) and in any case as well as risk-averse actors in financial markets there must by definition also be plenty of risk-loving actors present in those same markets (otherwise there could be no insurance or trade in derivatives of various kinds such as credit default swaps); and these more risk-loving actors could be quite interested in variable rate bonds and prefer them to fixed coupon bonds.

Therefore taking the evidence already cited regarding FDI flows and the above arguments regarding the inevitable presence of risk-loving as well as risk-averse actors being present in financial markets we may conjecture that the effect of one or a group of countries going it alone in adopting the banning of all interest on loans would certainly not be to wipe out inward loanable fund flows to those countries; at most it may alter the type of lenders and investors who may be most interested in getting involved in the financial markets of these countries. The dislocation or disincentives arising from such a non-universal application of the policy would therefore be likely to be fairly limited if not negligible.

The first major policy prescription as described above is negative in orientation: it says what is to be banned. A well-founded critique leading to practical implementation must also on the positive side show what can replace the banned activities. Based on the detailed discussions of Chapters 5–7 we have made some suggestions in this regard as to what can replace an interest-based system; and given that a financial system without interest exists in a more or less strict form already in Islamic finance we have drawn significant practical inspiration from certain Islamic financial practices. These positive policy prescriptions are different across the three broad classes of lending we have distinguished in previous chapters: lending to businesses, lending to consumers for current consumption and lending to governments.

Policy action 2: lending to business on a profit/loss sharing basis

Our second major policy prescription is positive in nature and relates to business borrowing. **Lending to businesses at predetermined interest** (debt financing) **would be entirely banned and replaced by a system whereby lenders instead of such interest payments would be offered a share in the profits *and* in the losses of the business venture**. Since such a system is already widely established in the form of *Mudarabah* and *Mukarashah* in Islamic financial systems there can be no doubt whatever as regards its feasibility. There is also of course *Murabahah* that is perhaps the most common form of business investment finance by Islamic banks but *Murabahah* looks very similar to and in effect is very closely akin to fixed interest debt financing. In *Murabahah* the business requests the bank to buy some equipment or real estate (or any other form of real capital) on its behalf and the business then repurchases the equipment at a mark-up defined in advance in instalment payments. The mark-up is defined as "profit" but being agreed and fixed in advance it looks very much like a conventional loan or debt financing at a fixed interest rate. While it may be true that *Murabahah* is in many Islamic banks the most common form of business financing it does not mean that *Mudarabah* and *Mukarashah* do not also exist and are commonly used in Islamic banking as well and so their feasibility is undoubtedly established.[5]

We have already noted in Chapter 5 how such a system of profit and loss sharing for business loans would have arguably beneficial macroeconomic effects insofar as in the slump phases of business cycles there would be significantly less bankruptcies. Not only would this ease the macroeconomic dislocation and suffering that occur in slumps it would allow perfectly viable and well-run businesses to survive, businesses which face hard times not because of their own inefficiencies or poor decision-making but because of the vagaries of macroeconomic forces. That is not to deny the significance of Schumpeter's creative destruction of firms during periods of rapid technological change; it is only to say that in periods of serious slump unnecessary extinction of perfectly viable firms can be avoided. Moreover if one is concerned about the persistence of so-called "zombie" firms which by definition are firms which manage to stay in existence despite no real prospect of long-term profitability (usually thanks to various forms of government support) it has to be said that under a profit and loss sharing system no investor would want to lend to such firms…unless of course the forms of government support that keeps the firms alive is projected to continue in the future. In other words it is not a system of profit and loss sharing that will keep zombie firms in existence but rather continued government support. That is not to say that such support is mistaken or somehow inefficient since there may be good reasons of public policy for keeping the zombies in existence to meet various social goals.[6]

It will be recalled that in Chapter 6 where we dealt with lending to consumers that we made a distinction between mortgage lending and student loans on the one hand and lending for purposes of current consumption (e.g. for a holiday). In the case of mortgages where an income stream is generated for the mortgagee either explicitly in terms of a rental income flow or implicitly (if owner occupied) in the form of rental payments avoided, such lending to consumers is for purposes of our argument closely analogous to business borrowing precisely because of the income stream and potential capital gain in asset value that are generated. Consistently therefore with our overall argument, **mortgage lending at fixed interest** (or at variable rates in the sense of following central bank refinancing rates rather than profitability of the real estate investment itself) **should be prohibited and replaced** as with all business lending **by a system in which lenders participate in the profits or losses of the real estate project itself** (including in capital gains and losses). Mortgage lending on such a basis will be completely feasible for the same reasons as business lending on the same participatory basis as argued above. In Chapter 6 we developed a closely analogous argument in respect of **student loans**: education typically increases earning power and so we can envisage the **abolition of interest on student loans and its replacement by**

a participation for lenders in any increases in income stream to students resulting from their further education.

The fact that a switch away from any type of fixed interest debt financing to a financing based on profit and loss sharing is technically and economically feasible both for business borrowing in general and for mortgages and student loans does not necessarily mean that switching to such a system would in practice be easy because there would undoubtedly be a huge resistance from various vested interests. Broadly speaking creditors of all kinds other than those who are risk-loving will seek to resist a system which would undoubtedly alter the power balance between lenders and borrowers and require lenders to share in risks. But since we have clearly demonstrated the economic feasibility of such a system it follows that the resistance is entirely political in nature even if creditors will try to dress up their arguments in terms of the drying up of credit and ensuing economic contraction. That is little but scaremongering by a powerful set of vested interests because if creditors do not lend in any form, well they make no returns on their savings/wealth; and for returns they are of course always avid.

In any case for more risk averse lenders there will always be other types of investment less risky in nature into which they may direct their savings. Individual savers can invest in improvement of their own homes while institutional savers can choose the less risky business projects or buy government bonds of governments deemed to be at very low risk of default. None of these of course are ever entirely risk-free and this underlines an important point regarding our proposals: their difference from the current interest-based system is essentially a difference of *degree* rather than of kind: lenders would bear more risk than they do under the current system but that is all. Putting the point slightly more colloquially, vested interests will squeal loudly and lobby assiduously by every means they can think of (and the financial sector is very experienced at lobbying); but if stared down by strong governments they will soon enough comply and move to lend on a risk-sharing basis since that will always be preferable for them to not lending at all. This is not about economic feasibility but about a redistribution of power.

Associated with such a redistribution of power some modifications to corporate governance norms and regulations may also be necessary. To understand these it is vital to recall a point to which we referred earlier in Chapter 6. Money (or loanable funds) is not per se a factor of production but it can be converted into a factor of production if when funds are advanced they are converted into a form of real capital whether material (equipment, real estate) or immaterial (know-how through R+D). In the schema that we are proposing lenders would be participating in the risks associated with any utilisation of real capital for productive purposes and so in a sense they would become passive or inactive entrepreneurs in effect. When considered in this way questions of representation in terms of corporate governance arise. In effect we can identify in principle three types of participation which are available to potential lenders to a business enterprise: (a) they can become full blown partners participating not just in the financing of the enterprise but also being involved on a day-to-day basis in management; co-entrepreneurs in effect; (b) they can advance funds and share in risks while taking a back seat type of role in relation to day-to-day management, for example through being members of a supervisory board of directors in publicly quoted companies and (c) they may simply provide funds without any involvement in the daily operation of the business, participating at best passively as non-activist shareholders. With each of these broad types of participation different levels of involvement in the decision-making of the enterprise may be demanded as suggested above and so if our proposals were applied in practice they would probably have significant implications for the role of lenders' corporate governance of the businesses in question.

Policy action 3: an outright ban on lending to consumers for current consumption purposes

Probably the most radical of the policy prescriptions that we have suggested is in respect of lending to consumers for purposes of current consumption. We have argued that because no future income stream arises from such borrowing by consumers (and still less any kind of capital gain) there is no possibility of a participatory set-up in profits and losses such as we have envisaged for business lending. Hence consistently with our central argument **no charging of interest of any kind should be permitted** on lending to consumers **for current consumption**. In that case lenders can make no return whatever on such loans and **so in effect such lending would disappear** given that other profitable forms of lending to businesses or mortgages would still be possible. It is true that firms in order to boost their sales when times are tough for consumers might offer deferred payment or instalment payment schemes but no surcharge could be applied in such payment schemes (nor conversely could any discount be applied for immediate payments): the permitted schemes would in effect be a form of lending at zero (nominal) interest rate to consumers.

Coming to the question of feasibility of this proposal in one sense it is certainly feasible: we could simply pass a specific law to this effect or if we follow proposal 1 above to make a blanket prohibition of the charging of interest on loans in all of its manifestations, this would already encompass the specific ban on lending (at interest) to consumers. The questions that might arise in respect of feasibility have to do rather with enforceability of such a ban and what it might mean for overall consumption in countries applying the ban. Taking the first challenge regarding enforcement one could wonder how in a society with any significant degree of individual freedom individual or institutional actors could be prevented from getting involved with interest charging on loans to consumers if both parties wanted to make such a deal or agreement.[7] Yet even in the more liberal of contemporary societies not every contractual agreement between individuals is enforceable at law: sales by people of their own human organs are typically outlawed, people may not sell themselves into slavery and of course many countries still have anti-usury laws on their books whereby the charging of *excessive* interest (interest in excess of a defined annual percentage rate) is illegal and so unenforceable at law. Now while it is for sure the case that neither slavery nor usurious lending have been completely eliminated by the laws against them (there are still usurious back street lending and payday loan operations with usurious rates) the fact of outlawing such practices has it is fair to say significantly reduced the extent of such activities and they are held in opprobrium by the general public in most countries. So while an outright ban on any charging of interest to consumers on loans for current consumption might not be 100% enforceable and may not entirely bring the practice to an end, it could be expected to have a strongly discouraging effect on such activities. Essentially such lending could only occur outside the writ of the legal system and would become a black market back street activity like usurious lending is today in most advanced countries.

The second type of challenge in terms of feasibility relates to the impact on current consumption levels. We have seen in Chapter 6 that the proportion of total current consumer spending that is dependent on consumer borrowing/debt financing of all kinds is typically of the order of between 10% and 20% of GDP in most advanced countries. Hence if consumer borrowing for current purposes (as opposed to mortgages or student loans) were abolished overnight by an outright prohibition as advocated here there would be an immediate collapse of consumer spending of the same order (10%–20% of GDP) and in macroeconomic terms that would represent a dramatic enough negative shock to aggregate demand of which consumer spending represents typically between 70% and 90% over most of the world. The effect would be admittedly quite varied being mainly concentrated in advanced economies and even among these there are considerable variations in the levels of total consumer indebtedness[8] that ultimately reflect very different attitudes and practices in respect of consumer borrowing. But because of the alleviation of the crowding out effect as described in Chapter 6, this drop in aggregate consumption would be partly offset by a rise in aggregate Investment demand so that overall aggregate demand will not be so drastically affected as the fall in consumption might suggest. Moreover the shock to consumption would be once-off; consumer demand would take one major step back immediately but would thereafter grow in line with GDP. If and when aggregate incomes rise then people will be able to consume more; but now instead of borrowing people will simply save until they have the money to make outright purchases. And here we revert to a significant point already made in Chapter 6: in such a world where consumers can afford to buy outright their various consumer goods without recourse to borrowing they would probably have considerably less personal stress and a healthier less frenetic and ultimately more autonomous lifestyle since no longer subject to the dictates of lenders and depressed by overhanging debt burdens.

Hence we conclude that although the proposal to end all lending to consumers for current consumption purposes is one of our most radical policy prescriptions it is perfectly feasible; and while for some countries there would be a short sharp negative shock it is easy to overstate this and in any case in the medium to longer term the economic effects would arguably be rather beneficial quite apart from and in addition to the Aristotelian moral argument: less crowding out effects and happier because less (debt-)stressed consumers.

In terms of vested interests which might be expected to lobby against this proposal regarding an end of lending to consumers for current consumption, the financial sector creditor groups would probably not raise much objections since there would still be plenty of mortgage and business lending opportunities albeit with risk sharing as under our second proposal above (and of course lending to governments as will be discussed below). If a vested interest would be likely to lobby against the proposal to end lending for current consumption it would be the retail sector. As advanced and later stage emergent economies become more materially affluent people's interest in acquiring ever more material goods wanes as a degree of satiation sets in and people turn to more spiritual pleasures. In the face of this retailers and manufacturers of material goods in search of ever more growth and profits have sought to boost continuously their sales by offering consumer credit of all kinds. They would be stopped in their tracks by the proposal we have made and indeed there would likely initially be a short-term collapse in consumer spending as the new regulations take effect. So no doubt there would be copious special pleading and lobbying from the consumer goods sector but as argued strong governments would need to stare down such lobbying in pursuit of the long-term common good and the psychological well-being of its citizens. Moreover as we noted the drop in consumption would be more in the nature of a once-off hiatus and consumer spending could recover as people saved enough to be able to buy the goods that before they might have bought on credit although over their lifetimes people would probably consume less overall. Given the well-known excesses of contemporary marketing and consumerism that might lead to a more balanced sustainable lifestyle for many people.

Policy action 4: government bonds with variable rate related to tax revenues

Our fourth major policy proposal suggests how lending to governments should occur in a system where payment of interest on loans and bonds is completely forbidden. **Lending to governments should be based on variable rate bonds where the return on bonds would be related to the rate of change of tax revenues of a country in relation to a base year** (which would be the year of initial issue of the bond). In Chapter 7, we have noted that a simple participatory arrangement such as we suggested for business lending (sharing in profits and losses) is not readily available here because a direct income stream such as would be offered by most business ventures simply is not present. But we also saw that at least some types of government spending, notably on public infrastructure projects or on countercyclical stabilisation policies can be expected to generate increased tax revenues via induced increases in GDP which could be used to pay a variable return/coupon on the bonds related to the buoyancy of the government's tax revenues. Since in cases where no induced tax revenue stream of any kind is generated there would be no return payable on such bonds there would be no (or almost no) buyers for such bonds we suggested **strict application of the golden rule of public finance**: governments should quite simply *never* borrow to finance such spending; and to make this distinction effective we suggested **a dual budget system for governments**: one separate budget for spending which even if desirable does not yield any tax revenue stream (directly or indirectly) and a second separate budget for spending on projects which can yield increased tax revenues through induced GDP increases. Only on the latter would government borrowing be permitted.

In order to give effect to the participatory return for lenders we actually suggested **a variable return that could be positive when tax revenues have increased for a particular year in relation to the base year of the bond; zero return when tax revenues remain static in relation to the base year and negative return when tax revenues fall in relation to the base year**. The exact size of the positive or negative coupons could be negotiable or (more likely) set by market forces in competitive financial markets: the only mandatory element would be a zero coupon when the tax revenues remain static.

In Chapter 7 we have already discussed in some depth the economic feasibility of such an arrangement so there is no reason to repeat the details of that argument here. We suggested both on theoretical grounds and on the basis of various bits of clear empirical evidence from bond market behaviour in recent years that such arrangements with more risky variable return bonds can certainly work; and we even suggested that this would be the case even if the application of the new system were not universal but applied only by certain countries while others maintained the contemporary fixed coupon system. We noted that market disciplines would readily ensure that countries would not fall into the moral hazard of constantly reducing tax rates and so (typically) tax revenues since the constant imposition of negative return by a country would soon mean that nobody would want to buy its bonds. The variable rate bonds will only be attractive if they regularly pay significant positive returns as well as sometimes negative returns. We also pointed out that the variable rate system for bonds would force governments to consider the long-term tax implications of their contraction of debt;

they would explicitly have to face up to Ricardian equivalence. This in turn would introduce a much greater degree of intergenerational equity across time in regard to debt financing of public sector spending. Under the current systems of bond financing with (positive) fixed interest coupons the payment of today's public sector debt is unloaded on to future generations who will not only have to repay the principal on the debts but also the interest/coupons; hence the future generation's burden will by definition be in excess of the value of the benefits represented by the current government spending that the debt finances. Although some economists may argue that future generations will be richer due to economic growth and so be in a better position to pay off the principal plus the interest, that argument is at best approximative (will the economic growth have been sufficient?) and leaves the fundamental intergenerational inequity of having future generations pay off a greater sum than was initially borrowed. That inequity would be largely eliminated under the system we are proposing. Moreover as a kind of cherry on the cake we showed how the danger of exploding government debt with ever bigger rollovers would be almost entirely eliminated since fixed interest charges/coupons are a significant and quasi-automatic source of rolling over past debts *at higher sums* at least in slow-growing economies.

It will be evident from the above that the variable rate system of returns for government bonds which we are suggesting would actually be quite attractive for governments in a number of ways and would help to instil a significant degree of fiscal discipline without implying stringent austerity policies. To apply strictly the golden rule of public finance governments would have to have two separate budgets as outlined above, they could still spend but only on the basis of fully funded tax revenue on the first budget while on the second budget they could have even quite large budget deficits. They would thus need to be much more selective in the ways in which deficit spending is used and to recognise Ricardian equivalence, the need to generate tax revenues in the future to be able ultimately to pay off debts and avoid debt explosion. From where then might opposition to such a scheme emerge? As with business lending on a profit and loss sharing basis it would be likely that financial creditors of all kinds many of whom are risk averse would mount a lobbying campaign threatening that with such a system credit to finance public sector budget deficits would largely dry up. But we have already seen that this argument is both theoretically wrong (there are no risk-free bonds and there are plenty of more or less risk-loving financial actors); and empirically falsified for example by effectively zero rate government borrowing during the Covid pandemic. Variable rate participatory bonds would therefore certainly be workable and so the resistance is entirely political in nature; it is about the power relationship between creditors and government debtors even if creditors will try to dress up their arguments in economic rather than in such brutally political terms.

A plan of policy actions

It may be useful to end this wide-ranging chapter with a summary of the plan of policy action in four key points as elaborated throughout the chapter. For each of the suggested policy actions we have in the above examined their economic feasibility and the likely source of political opposition to them from the lobbying of various vested interests.

1 **Following Aristotle's moral injunction promulgation and application of a comprehensive law admitting of no exceptions whatever outlawing the charging of interest on loans or bonds of any kind.**
2 **Lending to businesses at interest predetermined in advance and bearing no relation to the profitability of the enterprise** (debt financing) **would be entirely banned and replaced by a system whereby lenders instead of fixed interest would be offered a share in the profits and in the losses of the business venture.** All mortgage lending as well as student loans would be subsumed under this heading: **mortgage lending at predetermined interest would be prohibited and replaced** as with all business lending **by a system in which lenders participate in the profits or losses of the real estate project itself** (including capital gains and losses) while **for student loans there would be no predetermined interest** and returns to lenders would be related to the realised increases in income stream for the educated students.
3 **For lending to consumers for current consumption** (as opposed to for mortgages) **no charging of interest of any kind would be permitted**; in which case lenders can make no return whatever on consumption loans and so **such lending would in effect disappear**
4 **Lending to governments would be based on variable rate bonds where the return on bonds would be related to the rate of change of tax revenues in relation to a base year which would be the year of issue of the bond.** In order to give effect to **the golden rule of public finance** governments would be required to keep **two separate budgets,** one for spending which in no way generates any tax revenue streams and a second for spending where induced increases in tax revenues can be expected; and **governments would only borrow in relation to this second budget with variable returns to lenders as just defined above**.

Notes

1 As already noted in Chapter 7 on page 76 and footnote 9 in that chapter. See in particular the *Financial Times* article available at https://www.ft.com/content/56e4ddaf-dcf4-4a71–836d-b2d63eb9c2d4 accessed 28 February 2024.
2 See Investment Monitor (18 May 2023). *Where Are the Global Islamic Finance Hubs*, available at https://www.investmentmonitor.ai/features/where-are-the-global-islamic-finance-hubs/?cf-view accessed 25 July 2024.

3 Source for Figure 4 is UNCTAD FDI/MNE database as quoted in Islamic Development Bank (2022). *Annual Report on Investment Climate and Opportunities in OIC Countries*. Casablanca: Islamic Centre for Development of Trade.

4 See Chapter 6, p. 67.

5 See for example Banca del Monte dei Paschi di Siena (2009). *Islamic Finance in Italy: a €4,5bn Potential*. Monte dei Paschi Press Release. Siena: available at https://www.gruppomps.it/en/media-and-news/press-releases/islamic-finance-in-italy.html accessed 25/07/2024.

6 A good if dramatic example of this was government supports of various kinds to firms that faced major losses during the Covid-19 crisis of confinement in 2020 and 2021.

7 Radical egoists of anarcho-capitalist persuasion would of course hold that any such prohibition is immoral but that is a fairly fringe position. Most liberal thinkers will recognise limits to freedom of actions which may harm others including limits to freedom of speech.

8 See for example the table of consolidated household debt for the 27 EU member states, available at Eurostat (2024). *Household Debt Consolidated* https://ec.europa.eu/eurostat/databrowser/view/tipspd22/default/table?lang=en accessed 25 July 2024.

Bibliography

Banca del Monte dei Paschi di Siena (2009). *Islamic Finance in Italy: a €4,5bn Potential.* Siena: Monte dei Paschi Press Release, available at https://www.gruppomps.it/en/media-and-news/press-releases/islamic-finance-in-italy.html accessed 25 July 2024.

Eurostat (2024). *Household Debt Consolidated.* https://ec.europa.eu/eurostat/databrowser/view/tipspd22/default/table?lang=en accessed 25 July 2024.

Investment Monitor (18 May 2023). *Where Are the Global Islamic Finance Hubs*, available at https://www.investmentmonitor.ai/features/where-are-the-global-islamic-finance-hubs/?cf-view accessed 25 July 2024.

Islamic Development Bank (2022). *Annual Report on Investment Climate and Opportunities in OIC Countries.* Casablanca: Islamic Centre for Development of Trade.

Index

Note: *Italic* page numbers refer to figures and page numbers followed by "n" denote endnotes.

FSC
www.fsc.org
MIX
Papier | Fördert
gute Waldnutzung
FSC® C083411

Kolibri 360 GmbH
Ferdinand-Jühlke-Straße 7
99095 Erfurt, Deutschland
produktsicherheit@kolibri360.de